The People of Goda

By

Shani Oates
Maid of the Clan of Tubal Cain

Roodmas 2012

ISBN:1477481001
ISBN-13:978-1477481004
First edition, June 2012.

DEDICATION

To Evan John Jones, a true Godhi and member of The People.

My deepest gratitude to the People of Goda for their support and advice, especially to Jane &Arnett for making this publication possible.

TABLE OF CONTENTS

Preface

Mysteries Of The Cauldron

Right from day one the late lamented Robert Cochrane took great pains to stress the importance of the cauldron within the mythos of our Clan of Tubal Cain. As I found out later, this was not just the magical cauldron of the Celts that gave life to the dead etc., and a symbol we had drawn on heavily in the past, but one that came from a distinct non-Craft source. Superficially the clan cauldron resembles the Celtic one in that it too is concerned with life, death and rebirth amongst its many other attributes. However, behind all this lay another aspect of the cauldron. It became purely clan and even then its full significance was not fully explained. This was due to Cochrane's secretiveness and was never fully realised by me until much later. A lot of the basic mysticism and symbolism was based on a rather obscure and odd strata of what could loosely be described as early Thulist material. On one level of knowledge we had a cauldron based on the Celtic belief in a vessel that had the power to restore life to the dead and on another we had one that symbolised the beginning and end of time and existence.

On one level Cochrane publicly admitted that the cauldron mythos of the clan was nothing more than a synthesis of the old Anglo-Saxon mythology of the Norns - the three cave-dwelling sisters who watered the roots of the World Ash with water taken from the cauldron -combined with the Celtic myth of the cauldron as a vessel of life and death. But instead of seeing it in the same clear cut way as they did, we considered it to be the vessel or instrument of Fate and therefore something that we as witches must triumph over. ***When we eventually do Fate, the single name of the Gods, stops and the cauldron becomes still and the Old Ones are defeated.***

It is in this seething, restless ever-moving cauldron that past, present and future, all being one and the same thing, are found. We sprang from it and will return to it in death to await rebirth. That is until the time comes when we are able to face down Fate and death itself is conquered and we become as the Old Gods themselves. On a higher level, Cochrane said that Fate as symbolised by the cauldron is the cradle that rocks the infant spirit within it, sending it forth into life to grow a little in both understanding and wisdom and reclaiming it in death to await for rebirth. Magic and inspiration will eventually triumph with both Fate and the cauldron becoming still. The human spirit will then become a truly free being and as one with the Godhead.

This concept would certainly not be one that his grandfather would have recognised as being part of the traditional Tubal Cain mythos, far from it. His view of the cauldron would have been far more mundane than this. The cauldron would have been the pot that held the different bits and pieces that made up the pottage of the feast. It would have also been the vessel where the herbal potions and decoctions were brewed with very little spiritual meaning attached to it. For these people life was far too basic for many esoteric concepts to take toot. Their main concern was to follow their Old Faith and worship and work magic in the way they best understood, leaving the more high-flown concepts and magic to those occultists who could afford the luxury of holding and exploring them. This is not to say the cauldron had no meaning to them other than just a cooking or brewing pot, far from it. In the making of the pottage there was a realisation that the same thing happened with magic; different people coming together and sublimating their individual personalities and will to gain a certain magic result or end in exactly the same way as they have been doing for years.

It was Cochrane himself who expanded many of the concepts of the Clan of Tubal Cain with the proviso though that they had to mesh in with the basic tenets of the Faith that he had been taught. This is why very often some of his material seems to be very old and rooted in the past, while at the same time it has surprising modern overtones to it. So where did Cochrane's vision of the cauldron come from if not from a craft source? Part of the answer lays in the 1950s and 1960s when Cochrane first started to make public his adherence to the Craft. At that time, with so many witches coming, out of the woodwork, there was also a marked increase in books on the occult and witchcraft being reissued or newly published to meet the demands of this market. So it is little wonder that Cochrane, like so many of us, got hold and read such books. These in turn would tend to colour people's thinking when re-examining their own traditional material with a view to updating and expanding the basic concepts as in the case of Cochrane. The inherited material and concepts were basically sound and rock solid but also, as suited their time, simple. But who wants to stay rooted in a dim and distant past? Spiritual growth and awareness demands that the human spirit moves on along the spiral path of development or the whole damned thing becomes one pointless round of eternal sameness with nothing gained at all. Cochrane, like so many others, had to add to the traditional material or, like the dinosaurs, become extinct because it was no longer valid to this day and age.

"In the beginning the universe was a place of immobility, stillness and frozen non-existence". For "universe" read "cauldron" and then the concept goes on from there: "In the beginning the cauldron was still, no motion, no matter, no energy. Then the Godhead decreed the Primal Movement and the surface of the cauldron started to move. With this movement came the start of time, no longer was it asleep buried in the bosom of duration. With this primal movement time began and Fate began and the spirit of humankind started its long climb from the mud to the stars. Fate shaped the Old Gods and the Old Gods and Goddess in turn shaped us and held out the helping hand needed to lift us above the slime of the Primal Movement."

When the cauldron eventually becomes still - what then? Time will cease to exist, total stillness without any form or motion will become the norm and no motion equals no matter, energy, movement. This is summed up as :

"Energy-inertia-consciousness-substance-spirit-matter-Gods-humanity - a series of opposites linked together as mutually indispensable"

...until the Primal Movement brings motion and a state of flux to the cauldron once again or, putting it another way, reaching a point of Absolute Zero.

Evan John Jones

first published Issue #103, The Cauldron, 2003

Foreword

Who are the People of Goda?

"The Goddess comes from here"

(Roy Bowers)

Could there be a more enigmatic statement? In an intriguing document that sought to expand the boundaries of knowledge, conveying Craft philosophies experienced at that point in his life, Roy Bowers asked this of himself as much as he did the gods themselves. Placed emphatically as North-East upon a Compass Rose, it is entirely without context or apparent association to Clan Mythos. Discovering how this deeply embedded mystery actually relates to our cosmology became the task assigned to me by my dear mentor, Evan John Jones, to whom this book is dedicated. He wished to elucidate a certain vision; a perception of truth both he and Roy Bowers had shared. Having received an appreciation of these most profound beliefs from my mentor, whose arteful tutelage provided me with only sufficient guidance for my needs, I was hungry, desirous of more. The die was cast; I took the bait and ploughed myself into the work proper.

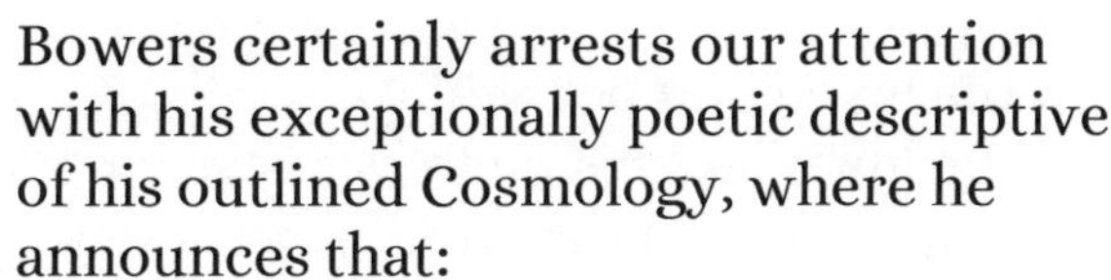

Bowers certainly arrests our attention with his exceptionally poetic descriptive of his outlined Cosmology, where he announces that:

"In the beginning there was only Night, and She was alone. Being was absolute, movement was there none."

Without preamble, we are led straight into the Three Mothers, the *Matrae Dei*, anchored firmly within the Iron-Age Culture of Northern Europe. Bowers expresses their qualities as Air, Water and Earth, teased by the distinction paralleled in the Hebraic equation of Air, Water and Fire. In a perplexing divergence between these two expressions, the spirit of revelation ascends in the glorious triple pronged shin as celestial fire, the spirit of the Shekinah and vital key to unlock this mystery. Bowers did of course quite doggedly insist that fire was the Promethean gift to man alone, stolen from the gods during an era preceding Iron Age beliefs and culture. Now lost within the hoary mists of the Stone Age, it is easy to forget that he made no comment that attached gender to this celebrated gift to humankind. No description assigns a masculine principle to this element, nor by extension to its deliverer or messenger; only the keeper, the wielder, is male.

In the advent of shifting phases of productivity, creativity within the arts and sciences, language, culture, music and poetry, it becomes too simplistic to assume a holistic apprehension of those deific spirits through whom these arts are a product of gyfu as suggestive of reciprocity of causality. We are all thus inspired to ever-greater things, to shift beyond the subsistence and saturnine boundaries of limitation and apathy. The Muse inspires all to succumb to Her embrace, and in sublime surrender become divinely infused hereafter, as one of "*Her darling crew.*"

But who is She?

I am what ye think me to be
I am what ye consider of thyself.
I am myself and thou as thou art
And will be……time come.
I am Robin, and more of that with less.
I am that without form
And that without force,
Yet form and force I be.

I am the loved and beloved
I am the lover and his mate
I am the whole and the part.
I am compassion healing pain
I am diamond cutting stone hearts.
I am a mirror without reflection.
I am the well without water,
From which all must drink.
I am words, love and words
Yea! but never speak.

I am pain, grief, sorrow and tears,
The rack, the noose, the stake.
The flayer and the flayed.
The hunter and the hunted
I am the head without a body
I am the body without a head
Yea! All this and still I am whole.

I am night and sleepless fear
I am fear.
Thou must conquer me to release thy soul.
I am peace, compassion now if ye understand
I am turned about, then turned again
Three times three, times 13 I turn
Then still more, and more
For the hare escape me not.
I am the dead, the living dead, the dead that talk
I am the born, the unborn, the completed cycle.
I am a root, a leaf, a tree

I grow upon memory of past, present and future.
All things are mould for me.
My top rests in eternity,
I am the breast of infant suckling [Fate?]
My loves kind embrace
Constant, ever demanding
Yet I be fickle withal
For all knows me and have laid upon my breasts
Yet few have had me and they are dead.
Secret I be, secret am, secret for evermore.
Yea, but a plated host marcheth at my skirt

For I am mighty as the berserkers knew me
My nostrils are full of the scent of blood.
For the dead are heaped to honour my rage.
I am weak as woman knows me.
In that is the fullness of my strength
I am desire,
I am love.
I am the first created the first of all Sin.
Behold I am She!

(*The Ash Tree*, written after a meeting in 1963 by Roy Bowers)

Clearly this lady is ancient, primal, a complex singularity, a foundation upon which the edifice and hierarchy of being is constructed; the root of gnosis and key to knowing thyself! Clarification and vision are the dubious rewards of the seer and the seeker of Truth; anamnesis comes at a high price. It is poignant, but it is bliss beyond all reckoning. Tearing down the bridges of obfuscation to follow a pathway that leads us all through things unimaginable and things many of us would rather forget. All serve to trigger the cognitive responses. As external catalysts for progression, all stimuli are noted, collected, stored and analyzed. We are dormant husks, blown hither in the winds of change; we are but shadows in the dream of ourselves; we are all one and one is She.

And moved thus, the search for Her begins amongst the connections linking the glorious constellation of *Coma Berenice*, the crowning glory above the *Headless Maiden* to Virgo and on to the Golden Fleece, the dragon hoards and the Cosmology of the Compass - all within the overarching Wyrd of the Ultimate Creatrix. Following the history trail is a legend primed in the wake of an undignified retreat by the Romans from these shores. The tale concerns the first ruler of an independent region of Northumbria[i] known then as *Bernikia* and that Ruler's name was *Ida.* Although chronicled as a King, it is my strong belief a Queen was sovereign there. As a feminine pro-noun, it is given to archaic goddesses of the earth spanning Europe into Asia and India and the Mediterranean including Rome and Greece[ii] and all islands.

It is here also worthy of note, the sacred mountain rising high on the plains of Anatolia, is similarly named *Ida.* The *Holy Kaz dağlari* overshadows the historical Vale of Troy, finding mention in the *Iliad* and *Aeneid.* For migrating peoples into Italy and India it bore deeply into a fused cultural memory. One hoary legend dated from sometime in the 8th century BCE retains a recorded memory of a fiery comet descending as a glorious maiden to seduce the father of Aeneas, the mythical founder of both Rome and Britain through Brutus. It is further intriguing to learn the name for this magnificent mound holds an empathy with the goose, redolent perhaps of a later template for the reversed, rather patriarchal Olympian myth of the maiden Leda seduced by Zeus in the form of the swan.

In Crete, images exist that relate to the cultural ties between these regions, affirming closer bonds than have been previously assumed. One particular myth refers to a topographical facsimile of that other arcane mountain of Ida, the Anatolian mother mound, (Mater Idaea), acquiring status as the place Rhea birthed the Mighty Zeus; it is also the same mountain where the phaistos disc was discovered. In India, another omphalos mound became immortalized as the mythical Meru. Which is to say, this is the great grandmother mountain of origin described in Vedic literature as the Nourisher, giver of Abundance and granter of boons. In later centuries and distant geography, she is revered by Germanic peoples who defer to the Mothers cognate to the Roman Matronae, the birthers of nations/peoples and Clans.

Chapter One

LAND OF THE MIDNIGHT SUN

"Attempts to see myths as somewhat imperfect forms of narrative have given way to the idea that myths are, in fact, not narratives at all. Myth in its living primitive form is not merely a story told but a reality lived. It is not of the nature of fiction, such as we read to-day in a novel, but it is a living reality"

(Malinowski 1926: 18).

Dream-Land, by Edgar Allen Poe

By a route obscure and lonely,
Haunted by ill angels only,
Where an Eidolon, named NIGHT,
On a black throne reigns upright,
I have reached these lands but newly
From an ultimate dim Thule-
From a wild clime that lieth, sublime,
Out of SPACE- out of TIME.

Upon the grave stones of two former Clan Members, Ronald White and George Winter, this final phrase was chosen to mark their entrance as wanderers of eternity. It is not insignificant! It does assert a cipher to their dedication of the long secret tenets of their collective works, even unto the Land of Elphame, of Truth, Love and Beauty!

The historical Irminsul was a solar- phallic pillar used in religious worship via the cultural practices of the early Anglo-Saxons before its eventual wanton destruction by Charlemagne in 772CE. It is possibly related to an obscure deity named Irmin, which is almost certainly an epithet of the Norse God Tyr whose runic symbol it represents. The Irminsul is similar to (yet distinct from) the Nordic Yggdrasil, the axis mundi (world axis) of man and the Cosmos.

Irminsuls are commonly an upright pole, crossed by its union of earth with the heavens, for this reason, it is often linked to the solar wheel or cross. Thor's Hammer among many other things suggests a stylized Irminsul, a double axe or labrys, in fact.

'*Midnight Sun'* actually refers to Thule Mythos of the never setting sun...

The Black Sun is, the midnight blaze – the hidden lamp, often perceived as the saturnine father, but also the soulful confluence of the Fates. As so many non-classical cultures regard the Sun as feminine, we may place a new perspective on its quality of tremendous value to those mystics and occultists who have long recognized where the Black Sun glyph mirrors the traditional Vedic Black Egg, symbolic of the 'Spirit' element - the Akasha. According to Kenneth Grant's Typhonian current, it is the Sun behind the son - in other words, the source from which our own spirit draws sustenance. Historically this source is the yearning to return, the homeland of the soul, the basis of so many myths and legends. This represents for we, the People of Goda, an opportunity to explore those fragments, sample their delicate and fragile aroma and in doing so, imprint within the mind, a blueprint, a map that will guide us home again.

We begin at the base of the tree, both literally and figuratively as we attempt to assess what the tree is, why it is there and what lies beyond its branches. Like Jack, we are driven by insatiable curiosity to climb dizzying heights to a place beyond boundaries others complacent abide. In times past, our forefathers raised a pillar in honour of their god. Here begineth the lure.

Irminsul is said to reflect Yggdrasil. But perhaps this is too simplistic a view? It requires an appreciation for finer subtleties by those who had once deemed such matters as intrinsic to their very connection to the highest status within the early Germanic pantheon - Tyr/Tiwaz. As a deity that primarily enforces the Law, balance is thus maintained between the Earth and Sky. Tyr is also the resilient boundary between those forces of chaos and order staving all potential acts of destruction. Tyr is presented as Warrior, Priest and Farmer/worker fulfilling all three societal roles.

She [and I say She advisedly, as the unfurling research will confirm] is the principle active force - the shaper of Providence, by whose reciprocity we sink or swim.

The platonic year cycle of approximately 25,920 years describes the pattern described by the Sun at the Vernal Equinox as it shifts backwards though the entire celestial arc of the heavens in the zodiac to mark its own end and point of origin. Each zodiac sign spans approximately 2,160 years with all 12 constellations (known also as the Twelve Halls of Asgardhr) totaling the great year. This current Age of Pisces heralds the emotive, holistic act of individuation for all humankind. If successful, the sun will begin advent a new platonic year with the Age of Aquarius.

A graphic depiction of the Nine Worlds in Norse cosmology, dispersed through three particular realms, each ruled by an aspect of deity that best reflects the transcendence and immanence of their interaction with the affairs of man.

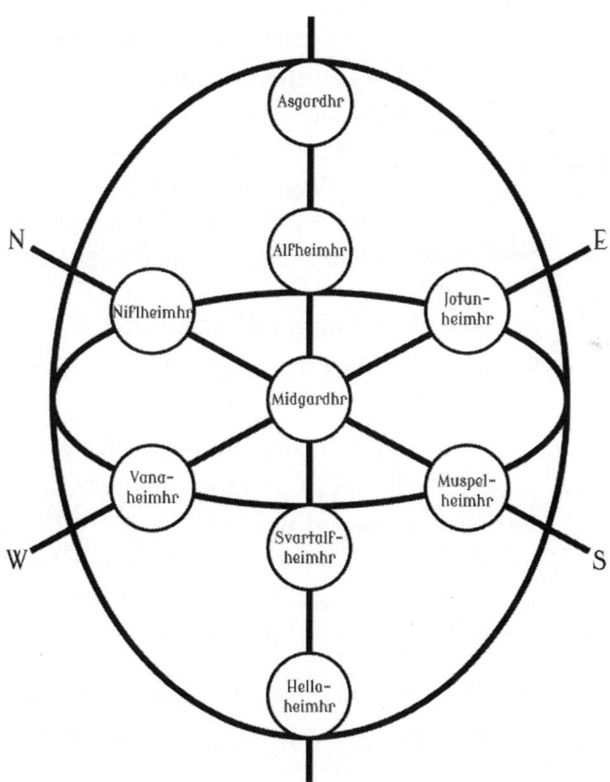

Asgardhr

1. Asgardhr-the halls of the gods - abode of the Aesir
2. Vanaheimhr – the dwelling place of the Vanir.
3. Alfheimhr – the world of elves, ruled by Freyr

Midgardhr

1. Midgardhr – realm of humanity - surrounded by the seas and world serpent (Jormungand)
2. Jotunheimhr – the home of the Jotuns, or giants.
3. Svartalfheimr – the world of the dark elves, an underground kingdom.

Udgardhr

1. Niflheimhr- frozen wasteland, eternal darkness, ruled by the Goddess Hella.
2. Muspelheimhr – the realm of the fire giants.
3. Hella – realm of the Dead.

The Nine Worlds

Alfheimhr/Elphame is the enchanted realm of the bright souls germane to folklore and romance ballads drafted in from historical literary treasures to preserve the word. Tentative, fragmentary evidence has survived that affords little beyond a leap of faith; confirmation seems a wistful enterprise. Although a few lines from the Volupsa, Stanza 2 do suggest a hint of it belonging to the bright alfar (elves).

"Ydalirn call they the place where Ull
A hall for himself hath set;"

The *Helm of Awe* is the representative force of all runes, combined into the eightfold star. Twenty-four bind runes compose this potent glyph and talisman. Often made of lead, they were placed upon the third eye by the seers/ess as she expressed the following declaration, a moot affliction and blessing used within traditional craft modalities, especially our own:

"I bear the helm of awe between my brows, the place of power: in my right eye I thus bear life and weal, and in my left, the powers of death and woe."

Irminsul – Pillar of Grace.

Tacitus wrote of many things in his histories. But in Germania he mentions at length the Pillars of Hercules, which he affirms relate to a tribe known by the title Frisii. Later in the 9th century, a stone pillar was unearthed at Obermarsberg [Westphalia, Germany] and relocated to the Hildesheim Cathedral [Hildesheim Lower Saxony, Germany], which may possibly support his theory. But, it is more likely that this pillar was the remnant of an Irminsul, a pillar of tremendous importance and religious significance to the Teutons. Extending this further, we can relate these tentatively to the twin pillars of Tubal Cain, the gateway to the sanctuary of Edin, the holy ground of the ancestors. Known also as the blood acre or divils acre - it is the sacred portion within the landscape assigned particularly to the devotional and religious acts of worship and sacrifice.

Given as the Nemeton, the sacred ring, the mound and the hollow hill, it is the point of origin, that is, the heartland of our forefathers. This becomes especially important to the discovery of information on the historical Thule, the thing and Thuringia! Located northwest of the Orkney isles: the mythical island of Thule was included on this 16th century *Carat Marina* of Oleos Magnus. On classical maps, Thula, Thila, or Thyïlea, is always a region far to the north.

Often considered a remote and inaccessible island in antiquity, it became assigned to the very real landscapes of Iceland or Greenland during the medieval period. More recently, suggestions place Thule as a group of islands either of Norway, the Orkneys, the Shetlands or even parts of Scandinavia. The medieval term *Ultima Thule* relates to a fabled land located beyond the 'borders of the known world.' Ultima Thule is also the name of a specific location within a Mammoth chthonic Cave system. In Teutonic lore, beautiful swan maidens lived in retreat within Caves obscured by trees in dense forests, appearing only to take up the souls of the dead. And of course we can only imagine how such a concept would have fascinated Roy Bowers whose zealous passion for caving is renowned.

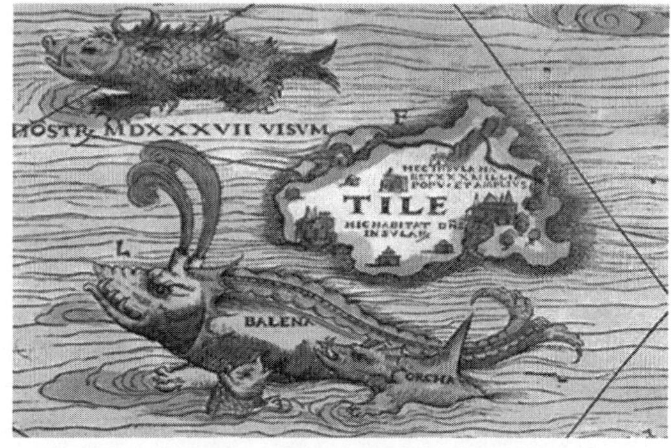

Under considerable pressure after Pope Boniface had ordered the destruction of their great holy gardhr tree, the Geismar Oak, the region of Thuringii finally capitulated, conceding conversion from heathenism. This wanton act of vandalism successfully demolished, any vestiges of former paganisms long before the end of the 8th century. Nostalgia generates a yearning to retrace ones roots, to re-kindle history and in so doing, it formulates a mythical history from song and legend. During the 19th century a manuscript appeared on the antiquities market purporting to be the Oera Linda Book of Frisian origin. It covers historical, mythological and religious themes from remote antiquity, allegedly compiled between 2,194BCE and 803CE. The manuscript remains as anonymous as it is absent of validation.[iii] Its intent is equally ambiguous. Such cosmologies remain intrinsic to identity and purpose within a faith, having their most purposeful foundation in culture.

Throughout this expansive period of history, the medieval arts and sciences flourished, gravitating to and around the massively cosmopolitan city of Nuremberg. Mythical links forged deeper connections from the Norns, re-naming it Nornenburg, where it is rumoured that upon Norn's Mountain, the arcane peoples of the Teutonic world still dwell. Clearly, the Vanir and the Aesir, and all the Great Clans and families of ancestral deities were subject to the whims of Fate, following faithfully the destinies meted out by this most arcane triad. All paid careful tribute to the immortal feminine.

Dreamland

By a route obscure and lonely,
Haunted by ill angels only,
Where an Eidolon, named NIGHT,
On a black throne reigns upright,
I have reached these lands but newly
From an ultimate dim Thule-
From a wild clime that lieth, sublime,
Out of SPACE- out of TIME.

Bottomless vales and boundless floods,
And chasms, and caves, and Titan woods,
With forms that no man can discover
For the tears that drip all over;
Mountains toppling evermore
Into seas without a shore;
Seas that restlessly aspire,
Surging, unto skies of fire;
Lakes that endlessly outspread
Their lone waters- lone and dead,-
Their still waters- still and chilly
With the snows of the lolling lily.

By the lakes that thus outspread
Their lone waters, lone and dead,-
Their sad waters, sad and chilly
With the snows of the lolling lily,-
By the mountains- near the river
Murmuring lowly, murmuring ever,-
By the grey woods,- by the swamp
Where the toad and the newt encamp-
By the dismal tarns and pools
Where dwell the Ghouls,-
By each spot the most unholy-
In each nook most melancholy-
There the traveler meets aghast
Sheeted Memories of the Past-
Shrouded forms that start and sigh
As they pass the wanderer by-
White-robed forms of friends long given,
In agony, to the Earth- and Heaven.

For the heart whose woes are legion
'Tis a peaceful, soothing region-
For the spirit that walks in shadow
'Tis- oh, 'tis an Eldorado!
But the traveler, travelling through it,
May not- dare not openly view it!
Never its mysteries are exposed
To the weak human eye unclosed;
So wills its King, who hath forbid
The uplifting of the fringed lid;
And thus the sad Soul that here passes
Beholds it but through darkened glasses.

By a route obscure and lonely,
Haunted by ill angels only,
Where an Eidolon, named NIGHT,
On a black throne reigns upright,
I have wandered home but newly
From this ultimate dim Thule.

by *Edgar Allan Poe*

Chapter Two

ANCIENT GEOGRAPHY

Scant fragments of literature survive penned by early Greek explorers that refer to Thule. Pytheas was the first to record Thule, though regrettably it is now cited only within the works of others. His lost scrolls told of his travels in the 3rd century BCE; though his descriptions fascinate still.

"Thule, those regions in which there was no longer any proper land nor sea nor air [earth, water and air], but a sort of mixture of all three of the consistency of a jellyfish in which one can neither walk nor sail, holding everything together, so to speak."

Later classical writers described Thule as residing both North and West of Ireland and Britain, possibly even as far as Iceland[iv] For the purposes of this treatise, the most fascinating thing found within their histories is a description of Thule as a large island (in the North) inhabited by twenty-five tribes. This may possibly even refer to Scandinavia, as certain tribes including the Geats and the Saami were listed. It was noted at length how several tribes returned across the sea to re-settle within that mysterious Island of Thule.

Sources in Ancient Literature

Virgil first coined the term *Ultima Thule* (Georgics, 1. 30) to infer a far distant place, unattainable, a legend; one of many to join the list along with: *Shambala, Meru, El Dorado, the Blessed Isles, Lemuria and Lyonesse, all sharing the status of ancestral mythical landscapes.* [v]But what is simply fascinating for us when studying the works of early Greek astronomers is the discovery of certain key words sharing a common etymological root that places Thule in an arctic environment, where the polar night becomes the romantic vale of ancestry:

'The place where the sun goes to rest.'(West/The Castle).

Summer nights on Thule lasted only two hours, a clear reference to the *Midnight Sun.* Another reference posits how '*Thule lies icebound beneath the pole-star.* 'Descriptions of the inhabitants of Thule are confirmed by later travelers circa 4th century BCE:

> *"...the people (of Thule) live on millet and other herbs, and on fruits and roots; and where there are grain and honey, the people get their beverage [mead], also, from them. As for the grain, he says, since they have no pure sunshine, they pound it out in large storehouses, after first gathering in the ears thither; for the threshing floors become useless because of this lack of sunshine and because of the rains."*

Thule, long held as the land of the Picts is given some measure of validation by later classical historians through a physical description by classical historians:

"... the blue-painted native of Thule, when he fights, drives around the close-packed ranks in his scythe-bearing chariot." and "The Picts are often said to have derived their name from Latin pingere - to paint; pictus"

A 12th century commentary on the Iliad describes them as small, dwarvish creatures resembling the legends of the Fir Bolg aboriginals of Britain.[vi] Other related legends from a slightly later period are sourced from within the Welsh Triads. Known, popularly as the *Matter of Britain,* they hearken back to tales of Arthur and his Three Queens, all named Gwenhwyfar (Gwenhwyvar). These continue to intrigue and baffle us, although I am much inclined to believe this enigma is more easily resolved if we view them as one queen with three aspects, aligning Her to the greater triplicity of the divine this literature expounds. The Great Queen is then represented within each of the three realms.

Literature attributed to Celtic language groups harnessed the power and virtue of the divine number three and its multiples; very similar to the Norse and other Northern systems in fact. Witness then fair Guinevere, as wise as she was ethereal. Her unsurpassable, otherworldly beauty stirred acts and trials leading to numerous abductions, rapes and abuses attested throughout all myths that centred upon her. Early traditions place

Mordred as Regent during Arthur's absence in the war against the Romans. But he usurped the kingdom, by seizing its Queen. Marrying Guinevere would make Mordred a legitimate king.

Although her main potency concerns the Triple Sovereignty of Ireland, the Irish Morrighan (*Eriu* and her sisters *Banba and Fodla*) enjoys close parallels with the Norns. Even the Triple Mothers are common to these myths. To become a true leader to his people and ruler of the land as King, Arthur must wed and mate with *three* goddesses to secure his claim to Sovereignty, expressed through the prosperity and continued fecundity of all life, in flora and fauna.

Battles are waged to effect his desire and in this, Arthur refers to his most prized possessions as: *Caledfwlch,* "my sword;" and *Rhongomyniad,* "my spear;" and *Wynebgwrthucher,* "my shield;" and *Carnwennan,* "my dagger;" and *Gwenhwyvar,* my wife; it is a noteworthy curiosity that all Arthur's possessions contain the element (G)wen or Gwyn,[vii] a standard determinative for white, sacred, pure, holy'.

Another, great queen of legendary renown is Mabh. Yet, despite a noticeable lack of direct references to her within sources that wax lyrical upon the facets of Arthurian Lore and myth, she is still a Queen of the *Fae* and therefore worthy of deeper investigation. Queen Mabh, also known as Queen Maeve[viii] features within Celtic lore revealing how her blood is the wine of intoxication, the sweet honey of the Beloved, the wisdom of ages fermented as Mead, the divine elixir – *aquae vitae!*

As Queen, it is alluring to note how her three attributes of nurturer, provider and protectress invite strong parallels with the tutelary spirits of the arcane lands of Sumer and of their instigations of Sacral Kingships. This emphasizes the gravid role of She who does not simply make sacrifice, but who teaches how and of what, a continuance of arcane lore and law of increasing relevance to this treatise.

Moreover, this recurring theme of the triplicity strongly suggests further associations with the *Drighton* whose generic meaning is given as (Anglo-Saxon) overlord through fealty. It is best exemplified within the Hindu *Trimurti-* Creator/Preserver/Destroyer. However, the Scandinavian word for Queen: *drottning/droning* is derived from this very title of *Drighton,* its actual meaning, given in its simplest expression defines both divine providence and execute. That is to offer sustenance [through and of] the sacred *art in officiating those offerings.*[ix]

In Scottish folklore, another Fae queen named *Nicnevin* is the Lady of Elphame, of the fairies, spirits, and all manner of weird and fabulous creatures that inhabit *'the Unseelie Court of Alba.'* She is the *Gyre Carline* and appears as *Habetrot*, a shriveled crone celebrated for her magical prowess with the Craft of spinning and weaving. But there is also a familiar sting to this hag through her ability to appear as a young and beautiful seductress. Cackling geese accompany her nocturnal meanderings as, wand in hand, her long, grey over mantle swishes almost silently across the icy ground, linking her to Hella, Queen of the Underworld.

Later branded as the Mother of Witches, the *great muckle Wallowa* her name became increasingly associated with witchcraft and sorcery. Interestingly, her name is linked through etymology to several cognates within the Norse pantheons as an *Ogress.*[x] This infers titanic status, certainly a pre-Olympian origin; possibly even a matriarchal status too. Rising from Hella, the underworld, All Hallows Eve is the night of Nicnevin, around November 9th –11th opening the gate for ancestral spirits to commune with their descendants.

Considerable ambiguity surrounds this dark figure of Scottish folklore, partaking of the characters of both Cailleach and Beira. She shares much in common with Hekate and Kali.

In folklore, Frau Gauden and her *four-and-twenty daughters* desired to hunt for all time. To Her horror, She watched, helplessly, as all Her daughters became transformed into hunting dogs before Her eyes. Since that day, it is She who now leads the Wild Winter Hunt casting Her steely eye over the landscape below. In similar fashion, both Holda and Bertha ride the wintery skies. Frau Gaude/Gode/Wode, as an aspect of Woden has greater legends to Her name based around the gathering of innocent souls, passed away before their time, usually, babies and small children. Through such descriptions we can begin to see the true nature of intrinsic principles in their establishment of a fundamental anchor germane to the core of all fables and sagas of our Northern Traditions. Twenty-five ride out on stormy midwinter nights, mother and daughters fulfilling the troth between humankind and the gods of old. As tutelary spirits they gather in 'all souls' lost in transition, they meter punishment and reward, they guide and guard through their elemental and visceral presence; this presence is their manifestation as the agents of fate, experienced as the winds of time and tide. These are the winds that whispered to Odhin the purpose they hold and of their individual virtue. And thus he named them in reflection of this realization.

With regard to the fabled Isle of the Dead, the great ancestral mound from which the Wild Hunt emerges, certain tales confirm sightings and experiences of great terror therein. An enigmatic passage in Chrétien de Troyes' Lancelot, or the Knight of the Cart, describes an encounter just after Lancelot has crossed the sword bridge to his Tower of Glass in the land of Gorre, which strongly suggests the fabled Isle of Glass. Another, very early literary reference in the 9th century Historia Brittonum uses the same motif to convey the troubling presence of a glass tower that appears 'magically' within the Ocean before weary travelers. This tale parallels very closely the Classic 'Celtic' story of a raid on the Otherworld to retrieve a Magic Cauldron, repeated in the *Preiddeu Annfwn* (Spoils of Annwn). Scholars have long ruminated on the possibility that these *Otherworld* fables are actually detailed records of very real attacks on Ireland that involved raids on early migrants attempting to settle there. In Welsh lore, an island to the west provides an explanation of the Irish name for the fortress, *Caer Sidi,* and of the difficulty of conversing with the watchmen on the wall as recorded in the *Historia Brittonum.*

These souls of the dead are revived in the supernatural cauldron but absent of the power of speech. Many of Arthur's treasures, including his wife Gwenhwyfar, were said to have come from the *Otherworld.* The abduction episode appears then to support a journey to the Isle of Glass, where dangerous passage significantly reduces the numbers returning to the Summerland's of the South and East. Indeed, Saint Gildas refers to the Orcades in the North, assumed to be the Orkney Isles. Orcus is also another name for the Otherworld.

This returns the thread neatly to Thule, that nebulous Isle, linked inexorably to the Dead beleaguered by the natural superstitions aligned to them. The Latin root *orc* signifies all things of death and the underworld and could sensibly provide the root of 'Orca'and also of' Orcus, that is She - Nemesis of those who renege their oaths. She is commonly associated with chthonic deities including Hades, Pluto, even Dis Pater. Its location is no less vague, always to the North and to the West. The Cave of Hella located in the Northerly Mound typifies the Northern European perception of the Underworld, guarded by a host of deities, demi-gods, heroes and arcane titans, the fey and elven folk. And so all points converge, returning again and again to a common thread, inviting a conclusion wholly compatible with the mythos of the Clan as expounded by both Roy Bowers and E. J. Jones.

The Myths of the Norse have preserved the earliest description of elves as: álfar. The status of the smith hero [hence the importance of this Craft to

Tubal Cain and his good Lady] Volundr became elevated to *elf*, even to elven ruler after his death. This becomes significant within the many Craft and Seidr related talents of Skulde, the youngest of the Norns expressed as the causality of her elven cast. Despite sharing certain physical attributes with humankind, their otherworldly qualities place them in the sphere of semi-divine beings within the cult of the ancestors subject to the animistic ancestor worship.[xi]

The Prose Eddas of Icelandic mythographer and historian Snorri Sturluson are responsible for our modern concept of light and dark elves and the Twin Vanir deities Freyja and Freyr whose attributes are personifications of those forms. However, this remains uncertain, as other scholars now question the numerous glosses imprinted by Snorri. More reliable transcripts are slowly replacing earlier works of questionable veracity. Eleventh century Skaldic poetry contains a curious verse describing an unusual encounter by a Christian who was refused hospitality due to the celebration of the *'alfablot'* around the time of the Autumn Equinox. It is especially interesting to note this matter of devotion to ones ancestors.

German and Danish folklore have more subtle things to say regarding their sometimes harsh ancestral spirits, who are similar, yet distinct from the Norse Valkyrie. Known as '*Erlkönig*,[xii]' she appears to those about to die. Their appearance assumes the mask that reflects the manner of death's embrace meted upon each 'recipient' according to their own deeds and accomplishments in life.

Described as shining, brilliant shades, of beauty unsurpassed or shriven hags of *grimma* dark. These are clearly experiences of the dark and light elves of Northern mythologies.

Chapter Three

ORIGINS: BERNIKIA: CROWN OF GLORY

The Myth becomes subsumed again in the histories of this beguiling yarn followed by painstaking research, arcane connections linking the reverence of the stars to themes veiled still in tales of a people whose voices remain in the Great Hall. To which Queen did they look to for the Mead, to whom did they call upon for protection? The heavens ablaze with the golden nimbus of *Coma Berenice*, the crowning glory betwixt heroes bold. This tells the Mound and the Maze, the Compass and the Point within the Wyrd of the One.

In returning to the history trail that begins after the retreat of the Romans from these shores, we discover the first ruler of an independent region of Northumbria[xiii] known as 'Bernikia.' Significantly, the Ruler's name was *Ida.* Although chronicled as a King, in reflection of all importances stressed thus far of the feminine principle affirmed by the beliefs of the peoples of the ancient world, it is my strong belief a Queen was true sovereign here. As a feminine pro-noun, it is given to archaic goddesses of the earth spanning Europe into Asia and India and the Mediterranean including Rome and Greece[xiv] and all islands.

When listing Arthur's twelve battles, Ida was referred to by Nennius as the Anglo-Saxon king of the Dark Age kingdom of Bernicia that is now the northern part of Northumbria. As Ida is thought to have had his court at Yeavering, there is good reason to believe that Arthur's 1st. battle, "*at the mouth of the River Glein*", was on the Northumbrian River Glen rather than elsewhere.
This map also indicates two "*Barden*" place-names and we believe that one of these was where his battle on Bardon Hill occurred. These are;
Barden Fell, 7 miles north of Ilkley, rises to 1544 feet(475 meters). and Barden (Hill) in Charnwood Forest rises to 912 feet(280 meters). The Charnwood Forest one is the most likely.

Kingdom of Bernicia

The Monarch of this illustrious region of the North founded a line of Anglo-Saxon rulers in Northumbria who further developed an extension of the runic alphabet already refined by the Anglo-Saxons being distinct from the Nordic Futhark. In fact the chronicles mention a Saxon Heptarchy of the British Isles, of Seven Clans, extant today through seven distinct Craft families. Research undertaken suggests considerable flaws in previous associations of Bernikia as a Brythonic province, highlighting a far stronger probability in the settlement here of peoples steeped in the traditions and culture of Anatolia. Sandwiched between the Pictish regions of the far north and those of the Brigantes immediately below, this coastal kingdom established a capital at Bebbanburg (later Bamburgh), which became the seat of numerous influential Bernician Bishops and a host of saints and martyrs, (namely Oswald and Wilfrid).[xv]

Despite obvious phonetic links between the Bernikians and the Brigantes, where both share geography and culture, not all historians are convinced and much has been dismissed that could assist our understanding of these early Dark Age regional Clans, especially with regard to their beliefs.[xvi] Even so, during these Dark Ages, language continued to fuse and overlap, resulting in so many variants of names and pronunciations.

Typically, those regions were certainly ruled by strong Queens. One in particular, Cartimandua[xvii], exemplary Queen and monarch of a northern British tribe known as the Brigantes is mentioned within ancient sources, specifically the Annals of Tacitus in which she is named - *Regina*. The other, Boudicca, appears exclusively in the works of Tacitus circa 51BCE. This infers a strong possibility that Cartimandua may have been one of the *eleven kings* that laid down their arms to Roman invaders under Claudius in 43CE. According to Tacitus, she ruled by right rather than through a gift of marriage. Her loyalty to Rome was unquestionable, handing over the rebel Caratacus in 51CE.

Sadly, original Romano-British places names are very rare in England making further topographical speculations untenable. Before the Anglo-Saxons arrived, however, Picts and other itinerant Northern tribes were romanised and some developed tribal kingdoms of their own. One such tribe, named the *'Goddodin', is* descendant of the *Votadini* located at *Din Eidyn* (Edinburgh). This tribe had previously inhabited territory along the coastal regions of Northumberland since and possibly even prior to the initial Roman invasions of Britain. By the 6th century they suffered increasing pressure upon them from invading Anglo-Saxons succumbing to inevitable defeat at Din Eidyn.

During the latter half of the 6th century, expansion across the North Eastern strongholds by the Chief/leader of the Angles, *Ida the Flame bearer*[xviii] from his *Kingdom of Bernikia* set the date by which a history of kingdoms known collectively as Northumbria, were established.

Sometime earlier in the Southern regions around Kent, another 5th century Anglo-Saxon monarch by the name of Hengest led a rebellion against the British King Vortigern – Nennius, said; "*from him are sprung the kings of the Kentishmen*" and *'Arthur fought with them in those days, together with the kings of the British; but he was their leader in battle.'* Bold and assertive, this comment affirms Arthur as *Dux*, but not Monarch around 547CE. Curiously, he later credits even this title to Arthur some time later, referring to him as: Anglo-Saxon King Ida to the year 547 whom we know already as the first 'King' of Bernikia.

> *"When they were defeated in all their campaigns, the English sought help from Germany .....until the time when Ida reigned, who was the son of Eobba. He was the first king in Bernikia,.. "*

From these auspicious origins, wherein Ida is hailed and invoked as a means of connection to ancestral spirits, undeniable links accumulate auxiliary momentum through discoveries drawn from sacred texts, especially those compatible to cultures with whom the Germanic peoples share their most profound ethics. Extracts taken from the Verses of the Rig Veda refer to *Ida* as the sentience through whom all sacrificial offerings (of Cow) taken become transmitted to all other gods. This establishes quite importantly her role and its context as the *deity of libations.*

> *"May Ida with her statute dwell beside us,'*
> *She in whose place the pious purge and cleanse them,*
> *She, the mighty, soma-soaked,*
> *whose foot drops fatness, meet for all Gods,*
> *Hath come to aid our worship."*[xix]

Vedic *Ida* is integral to the essential act of expiation germane to all rites involving sacrifice. In this sense, Ida becomes the woven mat of grasses upon which all offerings are given.[xx] She is also the pranic essence within oblations sprinkled over all participants in such rites that temptingly lead to conclusive similarities within parallel evocatory rites of abundance expressed through the Germanic and Norse *blots*. Again, this reflects the definition of *Providence* through *Drighton*, the divine abundance gifted through the Suzerain.

Chapter Four

ORIGIN & HISTORY OF IDA/EDDA/VEDA

All powers of perceived negative filtration to the etheric fabric of life is banished by the three primary mothers in the Vedic understanding of an inherent cosmology within the three primal rivers of creation (*Saraswati; Ida; Bharathi*). These are mirrored onto the body through its three vital channels, known as *nadis*, left right and centre. Ida is the feminine channel, coursing through the sinistral side of the body. Collectively, this triple *shakti* force encompasses the water/air/earth elements: *Saras*-Wisdom; *Ida*-Speech; *Bhar*-Devotion, respectively. It is also fascinating to note albeit briefly, that the dextral channel of the body is named, Shani, the Vedic Saturnine deity of stoic valour, truth, integrity, knowledge and obligation through oath. Its elemental attributes are fire/air/earth – precisely as Roy Bowers emphatically stated them throughout his published works.

Linguistically, female ancestral spirits, the Idisi are linked through their root to Ida, which shares further links in etymology with Veda and Edda. This fascinating company of related words expands to an extraordinary level, our appreciation of who they are and how they feature and to what extent, within the Clan's complex historical mythos. In their exploration, many profound points are realized that cumulatively clarify the faded gems and forgotten treasures eroded by time and circumstance.

Ida: name popular across the ancient world; not assigned to time or culture. Yet, its meaning did not change, from one side of the globe to the other. Strongest associations are given to the primal female; archaic [Germanic-]work/labour and [old Norse]-deed/action. Fascinatingly, the following list highlights the common root of *id/Id/Idunna.* In summary it could be said be best described as:

- *Ida* is possibly the name of the *Old Woman* in the O.N. poem *Rigsþul,* Rig/Rigga by others derived from O.N. oðr = spirit, mind, passion, song, poetry (cognate with O.Ir. faith poet; L. vates, seer, soothsayer)
- *[Rig]Veda* ancient sacred Hindu book, line 1734 = knowledge, sacred book, from root vid-*to know,* (from PIE base*weid-) *to see* (related to wit, and to Avestanvaeda *I know,* L.videreto see/vision).
- *Ida* The *flame-bearer* having associations with the welsh personage – Flamdwyn.
- *Ida* = Old German: wise/work/activity/craft: Arabic: a feminine principle relative to: foundation/base/to sit.[xxi]
- *Ida* is a female name derived from a Germanic word *id,* meaning labor, work. Alternately, it may be related to the name of the Old Norse goddess *Iðunna,* which means 'deed' or 'action'. It is also a Yiddish female name and an Old English masculine name, derived from the same Germanic root.
- *Ida* of Bernikia (d.c. 559) a kingdom in what is now north-eastern England
- *Ida* daughter of Corybas and mother of Minos
- *Ida or Ide,* the nymph of Mount Ida and one of the nurses of Zeus
- *Ida* (goddess), a goddess associated with expiation rites in Hinduism
- Pronunciation*: ɛdə (odel/oethel/ethel)*

Either of two 13th century Icelandic books, the Elder or *Poetic Edda* (a collection of Old Norse poems on Norse legends) and the Younger or *Prose Edda* (a handbook to Icelandic poetry by Snorri Sturluson) are the chief source of knowledge of Scandinavian mythology.

However, moving onto the *Three Mothers* we may again reflect and ponder upon their portion and purpose as a divine composite relative to the Clan tenets of Truth, Beauty and Love. The *Child* of the waters, the divine swan whose authority metes supreme Law, filtered through the element of Fire (represented by *Agni*) the supreme yet ambivalent force of all flame is frequently described as male. This association conforms to Roy Bowers insistence upon the three mothers being of *Earth, Air and Water*, with *Fire* as the domain of the smith god himself. It is of course distinct from the Judaic associations of Fire, Air and Water to the Triple Mothers, reflecting perhaps the disparate tenets of theology where one is born of fire predominantly, sustained by water, contra to the other, in which we are born of water, and sustained by fire.

In ancient Sumer, the Three Realms were of Heaven, Earth and Sea, where Heaven incorporates Celestial Fire and Air. In fact, the divine forces are drawn down from the heavens to earth, to manifest as fecund life, subject the Sacred Mè, the Testimony of Law and all Destiny through the primal goddess *Is-tar*. Another Vedic deity, Mitra may be related to *Itra* who is linked to the legendary Meru: Mountain of Origin and mythical mound of creation.

"... that Istar was associated with various locales is attested, but Istar smiles upon him with a placid smile, and comes down from her mountain, unvisited by man."[xxii]

Istar is the Celestial Mother whose area of influence in the Heavens is given as North-East, the compass direction for Edin, as asserted by Roy Bowers.

Within Hindu myth, poetry and scripture, all references to Mount Meru are expressed as residing North East! On a world map, from India and Iraq we can triangulate North-East. This falls upon Anatolia, specifically upon the plane and Mount of *Ida,* the holiest and most ancient of Mountains, the biblical location of the fabled Ark and suggested debarkation of the legendary descent of mankind. Here then, lies Edin. Thus *Ida*, the rock of creation, (possibly black meteorite) became the anionic Kybele. In this context, it would be appropriate to say that *Ida* represents the first known and oldest form of the divine goddess manifest and expressed directly through the element of Earth, given form and physical presence, acknowledged and honoured as such.

Biblical prophecy relating to the seven stars of *El* regarding the heavenly chariot, described by Isaiah as ascending from the sacred mound, have an astonishing parallel to the seven stars of the Great Plough, the cart of the Goddess as She travels endlessly around Her pole, as if bound by an unseen thread. These seven lights of *'ilu'* (virtue) are the seven lights of the celestial temple and the seven winds that dance around the Northern Star and Primal Ice Wind of the Frozen Hyperborean lands. This *Gar-edin* is the tree/pillar/mound/mountain of origin. In Sumer, this mound is named: *Kharsak-Kurra*, the *Mountain of the World.* Curiously, in Judaic lore, *El yon* means [specifically the *virtue* of] the Mountain of the Highest.

Ashmanu/Eshmun are the eight celestial powers united by the deity that presides over them, who is the *god* Sabi (seven). The prefix/suffix, *Il* (masc) defines power or imminence; this assumes another definition in the feminine form of *Ila/Ila* (fem) meaning the fructifying rains. *Ilu/Ila equates to Ida equates to* genderless – *The All* vented through acts of divine inspiration, spirituality, devotion and joy.

"Grace is the divine river that yields milk and honey"[xxiii]

The early settlers in India, commonly assumed to be the Dravidians, faithfully assigned their origin - *Ila/Ida* to the significant Compass point, Cardinal North! But subsequent Peoples, especially from more northerly regions, adopted and incorporated the emergent and evolving forms synthesized within the Greco-Roman and Germanic placement of their gods. After the flood, *Ida/Ila/Ilu* as the manifest form of *Vac* [xxiv] evolved into the Vedic goddess of Speech, Truth and Wisdom as first instructor in all the arts and outward form of oblation and supplication. Mead and honey were sacred to this goddess, whose strength through primal triplicity was said to destroy all darkness with light.

Within the affairs of mankind, there is one beautiful avatar, much beloved in Hindu philosophy named Vishnu. One of Vishnu's early incarnations as a Naga (serpent King) required him to advise *Manu,* [first of all humankind to survive of the flood] to consult *Ida* in all things. Thereafter, it was She who instructed him in the law of *rightful things* pertaining to worship, devotions and sacrifice. What is certainly becoming very apparent is the clarity of numerous links, previously obfuscated, between various sacraments and the preservation and expression of them through the mysteries, taught by a female deity to either another (male) deity, or to (male) humankind. It is quite illuminating to read of so many similar accounts of the female mysteries that echo the '*basic structure of the craft*' as we know it within the stream familiar to the People of Goda. Most significant of these pertains to the esoteric version of the biblical tale where Tubal Cain receives instruction on the valid method of expiation, propitiation and all oblations given up to the gods, through HER! These are the sacred female mysteries of the Craft.

All votive acts extant within the foremost religions of the world today are assigned and credited to these three (sometimes seven) early forms of the Ultimate Goddess of all realms, heavens, and the earth. It is She and no other, who taught humankind the votive arts of the mysteries, the prayerful acts of devotion and supplication, of libation and sacrifice, in all its forms. Once realized, this asserts a precedent for a re-analysis of the way in which we view the current sections of the Male, Female and Priestly mysteries.

Roy Bowers hints how the Clan maintains only two only of its original three mysteries, stating the loss of one as long lamented. Some have assumed this to imply the priestly mysteries, yet, elsewhere in 'The Mysteries of St. Uzec'[xxv] I have readily shown how Bowers never expressed that view; on the contrary, he stressed the *survival* of the priestly mysteries. It is in fact the female mysteries Bowers here mourns. Through vital nurturing by our guiding spirits the indwelling egregore, we have followed the well-laid clues and are now finally able to rediscover and reclaim these beautiful mysteries, now restored to their completion.

This Shakti force and Virtue had long eluded the completion of the works of the Clan. Form was given expression, retained through the priestly rites and paid forward, manifest though the actions engaged by the male mysteries of life itself. But the votive acts, the sophianic acts of devotion, the beatific spirituality has been greatly absent from the Craft. This gnostic effulgence completes via the triune mysteries of force, form and their expression through manifestation.

Hers are the karmic laws of the cosmos, the beatitude of communion, the art of sacrifice to the gods through innate acts of *gyfu*. Where such acts take place has been another subject of speculation for those seeking some understanding of the often obscure teachings of Bowers hinted at in his various letters. Now published these allow reasonable access for personal study.

In at least three letters the method described as - 'how to approach an altar' occurs, but first there is the need to determine exactly *what* that altar is! The following verse is drafted from the Rig Veda (III 4.8; VII. 2.8.)

"May the Goddess Bhavati [Ida],
In accord with the Bharatis,
Ila with the Gods and Agni with men,

May Saraswati with the Saraswati come here,
The three goddesses to sit at this altar seat."[xxvi]

Whence Agni is evoked, his sacral flame evokes the Three Muses/ Mothers. Language flux is again the domain of Ila, the very term in Sanskrit for expression of the Word, and Ila varta is a particular region of India held sacred to the goddess Saraswati (wisdom). Here a belief remains in Ila' as the teacher of mankind, the wisest of all sages. A hint/nod perhaps to the obscure Prajapati? It also means to pray, worship and energize. As Vac/k is cognate with Ida and even to Bharati, the word, and wisdom, it elevates, by default Truth beyond all.

Highlighted again, is the association with this term of the act of supplication – of the voice raised in sacrifice. Semitic languages also favoured L within the prefix and suffix el and il. The phonetics of language are clarified as recognizable patterns, emerging where later northern language groups transposed the l into d. Runic cognates have L - l, becoming D - d... An interpretation of this reveals the shift from the Void, the primal Mound, into the light and dawning of the new day. The demons of the darkness, banished by those of light, just as Vedic lore relates.

"Agni, the son of Ila is born,
We kindle you at the place of Ila,
The navel centre of the Earth."

Rig Veda III. 29. 3-4.

As the Morning Star, Venus births the Sun/Son, so then at the advent of the Winter Solstice; the Moon conjoins with dawn's light and Sun thereafter, celebrating a stellar, lunar and solar trinity within the heavens. This Vedic perspective sets a precedent for the numerous cultural variants that followed and built upon this premise, holding dear the veneration of the re-birth of a god at Dawn upon the Winter Solstice. Milton too refers to the Pale Leukathea rising as the Dawn to birth the Sun/son where further Legends relate how a white horse brings forth that Sun from the midnight.

Of course, this beautifully reflects the twinning of Mary and John as the winter and summer forces, although Mary, as Mother births the Christos; John is a mentor and priest (the Old Father) to the holy child. In this sense, Ila becomes the teacher and sage, initiator, passing over the means and methods of prayer and all acts of devotion. Forming the root of elegy, il actually means –to pray, the voice raised in sacrifice. [xxvii]

"where evening star and night come together"

Original attributes, associations, qualities and characteristics were transferred to other gods such as Agni[xxviii] and Indra[xxix]. Again we discover very interesting associations and links between *Deus* - divine/light/shining and to the original meaning of divine/day, combining as divine day light with particular relevance to our understanding of the primary hypothesis of Lucifer mythologically and theologically, the divine light of day, the solar day star [akin to others across Anatolia and Asia]. A deeper exploration of Agni's qualities specific to Craft, will determine this deity as an *impelle*r [xxx] that is to say, one who reveals the true nature of individual consciousness, of one's own innermost self through their light that shines within as the reflection of outer, the All.

This red Bi-faced god of life and immortality traverses the heavens and the earth, forging a bridge between them as the supreme messenger in his three forms as: lightening, fire and the sun. His energy is expressed as the need-fire, the friction of spirit in its evolution; the electric fire of the soul's potential and the solar, active fire of the body (of matter). Like Heimdalhr, his totem is the Ram. Seven rays are said to emanate from his body falling as the rainbow, the light of wisdom. [Bi-frost]

Rising from Her waters, wielding a life-generating Trident, the fiery triune shin - the symbol of the three fires She bestowed upon him taking manifest form as knowledge and wisdom, exultant through this divine priestly model. Twin to Indra who carries axe, torch, beads and spear, they begin to assert a dynamic oft repeated as requisite to balance and order in all subsequent monistic dualities.

Intrinsic to the Clan mythos is the importance placed upon the Pleiades, the seven mysterious sisters of arcane myth cognate with the seven hathors and the seven faerie godmothers of numerous heroes and demi-gods. Vedic lore cites Agni as a child born of these Seven Queens of Heaven. Of course, Heimdalhr in myth, claims seven mothers. These principles become filtered culturally and cross-pollinated such that similarities become easily recognizable. The Valkyrie present in their original duties at least, a cognate occurrence, further mirrored within the Anglo-Saxon and Germanic tribes peoples through the ancestral *Disir*.

Idis (Germanic)

The Germanic /Old Saxon *Idis* (pl *Idisi*) describes a divine being whose gender is decidedly female. Idis is cognate to Old High German *it is* and Old English *ides*, meaning 'well-respected and dignified woman.' Recent scholarship presumes similarities between the *Idisi* and the North Germanic *Disir*, Teutonic ancestral spirits deemed to have associations with fate as further suggested in the term - *Idisi*aviso (meaning *plane of the Idisi*) where the armies of the North fought with those of Rome around the beginning of the first century. By default, favourable comparisons to the Norse Valkyrie have been made and asserted.

One of the two Old High German Meresburg Incantations call upon female beings—*Idisi*—to bind and hamper an army: [xxxi]

The incantation reads:

'Once the Idisi sat, sat here and there,
some bound fetters, some hampered the army,
some untied fetters:
Escape from the fetters, flee from the enemies.'

In line 1259 of the Beowulf epic, in keeping with the increasing association of *Ida* with the archaic, primal and divine feminine, Grendel's Mother is introduced as an *ides*:

... Grendles modor
ides, aglæcwif ...

With regard to the similarities between the principle of the *ides* and *Disir*, the former may have easily become a term used to denote a type of [ancestral] goddess.

"Several of the Eddic sources might lead us to conclude that the Disir were Valkyrie-like guardians of the dead, and indeed in GudrunarkvidaI 19 the Valkyries are even called Herjans Disir 'Odin's Disir."

The Disir are referred to, rather prejudicially, as dead women in Atlamal 28. A secondary belief which states that the Disir were merely the souls of dead women (fylgjur) similarly underpins the land Disir of Icelandic folklore.

Simek says*: "as the function of the Matrons was also extremely varied – fertility goddess, personal guardians, but also warrior-goddesses – the belief in the Disir, like the belief in the Valkyries, Norns, and matrons, may be considered to be different manifestations of a belief in a number of female demi-goddesses."* [xxxii]

Fascinatingly, we learn that Zeus is said to have raped one of the Seven Sisters of the Pleiades, and She is the one whose son died. In despair at the horrors of man's inflictions upon one another, She retreated to the North as the starry constellation where it is said She loosened her hair and remained in mourning. Could this be another connection to the original seven Valkyrie? Or better yet, to Coma Berenice, the head of the Maiden (Virgo) of fecund wisdom in Medusa's mane of the flaming tresses of Ida, the golden fleece that once hung upon the tree in the gardhr-edin of the Hesper-ides? We could tentatively interpret this as the arcane wisdom of the Creatrix, the birther and mother of all peoples stemming from the source, the tree of life within the western Garden of Eden, the isle of ancestral spirits.

Chapter Five

HALLS OF THE GODS.

According to Snorri Sturluson, Asgardhr is home of the Aesir god, Odhin as Chief over his people. Being a devout Christian, Snorri is required to explain the sagas though an ethical and religious filter that transcribes and orders a system that is, in fact, alien to it. But not all historians support this; others assert that Odhin was never referred to as *All Father* until after their conversion to Christianity.

Through the writings of scribes such as Snorri the gods became translated into ancestral heroes of old where the twelve fabled Halls of Heaven are placed in the realms of a mythical landscape in a time prior to their migrations and Diasporas. That these strongly suggest the very principle of merit underpinning *Thule* is too pertinent to ignore. In the Poetic Edda, Snorri synthesizes the few scattered references to Asgardhr with imagery expressed through elements from within the Skaldic songs preserved within the Poetic Eddas.

Snorri explains the origins of the Proto-Germanic peoples of Northern Europe as sourced from the Aryan peoples of Asia. His conviction forges a link to them as the Aesir, naming Asgardhr as the capital city of a Homeland that is entirely based in historical sources. He confidently names this global centre as Troy, establishing a context and primacy for his promotion of the Halls of the Gods therein upon the *Plain of Ida*. And yet, for all other veils Snorri layers over his sources; in this line of investigation, there is a trail worthy of pursuit.

Moreover, within this prologue a certain king of *Tyrkland* is mentioned, specifically with regard to Odhin's descent. In time, it is the sons of Odhin that populate Northern Europe. *Yngvi,* became founder of the *Yngling*ar, an early royal family of Sweden, ultimately to become the main people to populate northern England.

In the Eddas, legends of these families of heroic beings and their interactions with the living begin with decisions considered and debated in the '*thing*' held daily by them in the As-Gardhr (Old Norse: 'Ásgarðr'- meaning the yard or enclosure of the spirits which is not an earthly place). Here also at the foot of the Great World Tree, Yggdrasil, The Norns determine the Fate of all, from all humankind and all classes of beings between them and the High God of all. Thirteen Valkyrie maidens are listed as those who choose their own from among the slain. Of course, there is also Odhin to consider. His numerous epithets form a composite of the many attributes he assumes over time from other deities that precede him.

Odhin: Alfaðir, Alföðr–All-Father.

But more interestingly, as Aldaföðr he is the 'Father of Men'.[xxxiii]

And thus, accompanied by his two ravens, Odhin wanders far and wide. Yet as a man, Odhin is fated to die. But, in this humanization of a 'god', Snorri created a problem that proved difficult to solve. For if Ásgardhr is here on earth, then where shall Odhin rest? Snorri resolves it by creating an alternative afterlife within a heathen ancestral homeland. Though some scholars have found problems with this view, I have to agree with its insightful and astute interpretation. It highlights a mythologized Cosmology innate within Clan based Peoples, especially where subject to filial and feudal auspices.

Later, a significant shift in perception developed the previous description of a fractured, cosmopolitan society into one that established its religion subject to a Sovereign statehood. Certainly, I believe it had been their understanding that each person possessed the kinetic virtue of ancestry. Therefore all potential expression and generation through a given social structure and religious enterprise established the arcane principle of the *Thing*; where all matters are known, and where whatever is 'necessary is resolved. This highly principled society held fast to oaths, allegiances, and *gyfu*; where the reciprocity of fate and fortune as the natural and organic measure of farming and livestock became the means of moveable wealth.

The Venerable Bede, a Christian Monk (of Saxon heritage) who chronicledthe Histories of the 6-7th centuries, noted the Saxon Calendrical celebration of '*Modraniht'* as its most Holy Night. Held at the Winter Solstice, denoting the importance as the boundary between one year and the beginning of the next, it was aligned to the birth of the new and waxing Sun. To those early settlers to the Isles, the sun and moon and stars were highly esteemed, reflected in their lunar/solar calendar. Other celebrations mentioned by Bede, follow closely the folk calendar extant through the preservation of lore and customs, however quaint or alien to our modern sensibilities.

Solmonað (February), Bede claims that special cakes were given to Saxon deities.

Eostur-monath Aprilis (April) spring festival was celebrated, dedicated to the goddess of the Spring Dawn.

Though not a goddess, it is of interest to note Grimm's speculation that regards this name as close enough to the east wind and a *spirit of light* named *Austri* (simply means East) recorded in the 13th century Icelandic *Prose Edda*: *Gylfaginning* to be a Goddess of the same name. It is ultimately sourced to the dawn, the breaking liminality of light.[xxxiv]

September was known as *Halegmonath*, meaning *Holy Month*, indicating a special religious significance.

November was known as *Blod-Monath*, meaning *Blood Month*, associated with the winter slaughter of livestock - an offering to their gods and food for Kith & Kin through the harshest season.[xxxv] Sacrifice of this nature was quite common during the early medieval period to the few remaining Germanic Pagans scattered across England and Europe. In Scandinavian countries, a similar sacrifice was named the *Blot*. This entailed a specialized communion Houzle, made sacral through the blood-honouring of the beast sacrificed.[xxxvi]

Bede's original Old English:	Modern English translation:
Se mónaþ is nemned on Léden Novembris, and on úre geþeóde blótmónaþ, forðon úre yldran, ðá hý hǽðene wǽron, on ðam mónþe hý bleóton á, ðæt is, ðæt hý betǽhton and benémdon hyra deófolgyldum ða neát ða ðe hý woldon syllan.	*"This month is called Novembris in Latin and in our language the month of sacrifice, because our forefathers, when they were heathens, always sacrificed in this month, that is, that they took and devoted to their idols the cattle which they wished to offer."*

As previously attested, the Cult of Kingship at the heart of pagan Anglo-Saxon society placed the King in the role of priest and warrior to his people. In fact, as the core tenet, it was deemed that he carried and held the Virtue or *haminja* of the people. Their Fate and good fortune depended entirely upon his judgment by the Fates as *Worthy* and as *Just.*

This principle is well attested within the poetic epic – Beowulf.[xxxvii]

Even the Venerable Bede stated how Heathens perceived '*life and death as being like the experience of a sparrow who flies out of a freezing night into a warm hall full of feasting and merriment, and then out into the night again'.*

Hrêðe/Hretha(OE), -the famous or the victorious) is another divine feminine quality connected by Anglo-Saxons to the month Hrēdmōnath. Hrêðe is attested solely by Bede in his 8th century work *De temporum ratione.* Her name appears in Bede's Latin manuscript as Rheda, it is reconstructed into Old English as Hrêðe and is sometimes even Anglicized as *Hretha, Hrethe, or Hrede*. Hrēdmōnath is one of three events that refer to Anglo-Saxon deities in their calendar; the other two being *Ēostur-monath* in March/April and *Mōdraniht* in December as above.

Yngvi, *Yngvin, Ingwine, Inguin* are names that relate to an older theonym Ing and which appear to have been the older name for the god *Freyjr* (an epithet meaning: Lord). *Ingwaz* is a Proto-Germanic deity, who as one of the three sons of *Mannus,* is the legendary ancestor of the *Ingaevones.*

Eventually, Latin/Roman names replaced many names used in common parlance.[xxxviii]

Very little of what we actually assume concerning the myths, legends, beliefs and laws relating to Anglo-Saxon paganism is due to the rather romantic, though often insightful accounts of 19th century poets and antiquarians. Largely they posit a natural animism base upon which a shamanic interaction is forged between the land and the polytheistic domain of the heavens above.

Though heavily focused around the worship of deities, they are known by their Clanic associations of the *ése* (singular *ós*) and the Vanir; other entities/classes of being frequent the realms of variable manifestation and pre-eminence, including dragons and elves. These magico-religious beliefs infurred a bearing upon the hierarchical structure of Anglo-Saxon society wherein kings claimed direct ancestral lineage from a particular

Tutelary deity, particularly of Woden/Votan. This in turn, influenced all Law and its enforcements through meted justice.

Elemental and planetary qualities assigned via this culture-based religion were provided with a basic template upon which their deific names related to each weekday within the English language. Although little is properly understood of Anglo-Saxon Cosmology, hints within the Nine Herbs Charm suggest a comparable system possibly derived from cognate studies of Seven Realms of Heaven. Stars and other celestial bodies are granted a similar importance, especially with regard to '*Earendel* which tentatively translates as the Light of the Morning Star. Pagan Anglo-Saxons revered a sacred pillar, though its significance to them is much disputed as being a cognate to the later Norse Ygdrassil. They are utterly different in their composition, application, religious associations and their cultural relevance.

As heirs to an Indo-European cultural system, Anglo Saxons maintained the 12 sectional sky zones as the vainglorious zodiacal belt, though with some interesting surprises (hinted within the *Vafþrúðnismál*).Further associations are accorded between Venus and Mars and Mercury. Fascinatingly, the world serpent *Niðhöggr* replaces the constellation of Scorpio. This may posit a worldview that embraced the stars as objects of divine account, rather than the planetary representatives named for them, typical within Greco-Roman perceptions of astrological bodies. If true, then *Odhin* is well aspected through Mercury as the Wanderer.

Tacitus may inadvertently affirm this in his report of meetings taking place according to the position of planets and of the moon in particular. He even mentions the importance they give to the divine twins named by him as Castor and Pollux that almost certainly refer to Hengest and Hretha. Both (Alcis) are alluded to in the *Grímnismál* saga. An enigmatic passage from within the Poetic Edda describes the World Tree Yggdrasil: its three roots, the three worlds; the eagle, and a serpent below that gnaws its roots; a squirrel and four deer that nibble the tree's foliage. In a 17th century manuscript (AM 738 4to) astrological associations that align themselves to that poetic descriptive are suggested pictorially. If we study the four harts and their names, we discover in them the hint of the monthly course of the moon through its four main stages with that of the annual cycle of growth of the deer: *Dáinn* = deceased; *Dvalinn* = the loiterer; *Dúneyrr* = downy ear and *Dýraþrór* = the waxing of deer. More importantly, they are also aligned to the cardinal directions.[xxxix]

Relationships between the planets and other bodies including sun and moon as well as other phenomena all react and interact through the very fabric of Wyrd to inspire the Skalds to weave and dart their movements into the great Sagas; for with each telling, another alignment to those phenomena forges another link in time to the eternity of Orlog.

"..aspects of behaviour express, if not as clearly, the specific phrasing of reality which each culture makes for itself."[xl]

In his study of identifiable responses by the human mind, Claude Levi-Strauss formulated a theory that observes our inherent interaction through environment with visionary stimuli generated by cultural myth. Levi-Strauss concluded that the *Mind* as its own creative Muse, the *esprit* structures the means of its own self-perpetuating belief. Those impressions then become an influential model of feedback into human activity.

"The vocabulary [i.e. outward manifestation] matters less than the structure. Whether the myth is recreated by the individual or borrowed from tradition, it derives from its sources--individual or collective (between which interpenetrations and exchanges constantly occur)--only the stock of representations with which it operates. But the structure remains the same. If we add that these structures are . . . few in number, we shall understand why the world of symbolism is infinitely varied in content, but always limited in its laws. There are many languages, but very few structural laws which are valid for all languages. A compilation of known tales and myths would fill an imposing number of volumes. But they can be reduced to a small number of simple types if we abstract, from among the diversity of characters, a few elementary functions."

(Levi- Strauss 1967: 199)

This is of prime importance in the pursuit of any heritage intrinsic to who we are.

Chapter Six

CREATION

Concerning the creation of the world, the Northern skalds or poets, whose songs are preserved in the Eddas and Sagas, declared that in the beginning, when there was as yet no earth, nor sea, nor air, when darkness rested over all, there existed a powerful being, an ineffable Creatrix. The following description reads straight off the page of Roy Bowers' Cosmology. In the center of space there was, in the morning of time, the yawning abyss called Ginnunga-gap, enveloped in perpetual twilight. In the freezing chill of the North lies the murky land of mists of Niflheimhr, but from within the centre, there bubbled the never ceasing fresh water fountain. This great pool, was aptly named Hvergelmir, the seething cauldron, whose waters supplied twelve great streams known as the Elivagar.

Ice formed in the biting winds, hardening like rock, rolling like thunder crashing against themselves, blasting the earth with sound. South of this dark chasm, and directly opposite Niflheimhr, the realm of mist lies another world called Muspelheimhr, the home of elemental fire, where all was warmth and brightness guarded by Surtr, the flame giant. This giant fiercely brandished his flashing sword sending forth great showers of sparks that fall hissing upon the icy blocks within the bottomless abyss, partially melted by their heat.

As the steam arose in clouds, again the prevailing cold transformed it into rime or hoar frost, which, layer by layer, began filling the belly of the abyss. The will of the seen and the unseen molded this endless cycle of condensation, generating a gigantic creature named Ymir or Orgelmir (seething clay). This personification of the frozen ocean drew life amidst the abyss as Hrim-thurs or ice giant.

"In early times,
When Ymir lived,
Was sand, nor sea,
Nor cooling wave;
No earth was found,
Nor heaven above;
One chaos all,
And nowhere grass."

[SÆMUND'S EDDA (Henderson's tr.)]

Groping about in the gloom in search of something to eat, Ymir perceived a gigantic cow, Audhumla, the nourisher, created from similar elemental forces. Ymir noticed with delight that four great streams of milk flowed from her udders. Taking his fill, he fell fast asleep. Looking about her for food, Audhumla began to patiently lick the salt from the enormous ice block close by with her rough tongue until eventually, Buri (the producer), now free, stepped forth. Thus from the sleeping Ymir, the world of man was created.

"Of Ymir's flesh
Was earth created,
Of his blood the sea,
Of his bones the hills,
Of his hair trees and plants,
Of his skull the heavens,
And of his brows
The gentle powers
Formed Midgardhr for the sons of men;
But of his brain [Goda means mind]
The heavy clouds are
All created."

[NORSE MYTHOLOGY (R. B. Anderson)]

Odhin, the leading spirit, now bade his descendants follow him to the broad plain called *Ida*wold, far above the earth, on the other side of the great stream Ifing, whose waters never froze. In the very center of Asgardhr (home of the gods), the twelve Æsir (gods) and Asynjur, better known as the 24 wind goddesses all assembled. Here in this sacred, hallowed space they decreed that no blood should ever be shed within the limits of their realm, peace, and that harmony must reign there forever.

They established a forge where they fashioned all their weapons and tools required to build magnificent palaces of precious metals, where they lived for many long years in a state of perfect happiness called the Golden Age.

"The Golden Age is that which exists in every moment: each stage of life from one obstacle of Wryd to the next is the Golden Age; each obstacle allows Munnin/after-thought [memory] to hold the lessons learned so that we become better armed to face the next obstacle. Thus are we honed, tempered and annealed towards and throughout the next obstacle in Wyrd. By living in the rightness of things, in balance and harmony, each of us may self-fulfill our own Golden Age. Each individual has to choose between order and chaos, to properly use Huggin/fore-thought to approach their Wyrd. The aim is for everyone to achieve his or her Golden Age collectively."[xli]

We may draw clear and obvious parallels between Huggin and Munnin as cognates for Prometheus and Epimetheus respectively.

The Realm of Man

Midgardhr, or Manaheim: assigned to humankind, yet created by the gods. Three mighty roots of Yggdrasil, the Tree of Life, formed deep within the earth, reaching into those other worlds of the gods, both below and above the abode of man. In Niflheimhr bubbles the spring Hvergelmir, which is all thought. In Midgardhr too, near *Mimir*'s well (as the great seas, which is all memory), and in *Asgardhr*, a third emerges close to the *Urdhr* fountain of youth, the cycle of all life and death. To maintain the longevity of Yggdrasil, the Norns daily sprinkle it with the holy waters from Urdhr's fountain. As this water trickles down to earth, it supplies the bees with honey and all thrive under its aegis.. From either edge of Niflheimhr, arching high above Midgardhr is the bridge of the gods, Bifröst (Asabru, the rainbow), composed of *fire, water, and air.*

Wives of Odhin:

Jörd (Erda/Urdhr/Nerthus), raw earth, daughter of Night/ogress Mother of Thor, the god of thunder.

Frigga, a personification of the civilized world. Mother of Baldr, the gentle god of spring, Hermod, and Tyr.

The third wife was Rinda (similar to Bede's *Rheda*?), a personification of the hard and frozen earth, who reluctantly yields to his warm embrace, but finally gives birth to Vali, the emblem of vegetation.

Odhin is also said to have married Saga or Laga, the goddess of history.

His other wives were Grid, the mother of Vidar;

Gunlod, the mother of Bragi;

Skadi; and the nine giantesses who simultaneously bore Heimdalhr.

All these ladies play parts in varying degrees of import within the numerous myths of the Northern traditions. [Eigg, Sigi, Skiold, Sæming, and Yngvi became *Kings* of East Saxony, West Saxony, Franconia, Denmark, Norway, and Sweden] From these Kings the legendary descent of the Saxons may be sourced and traced through Hengest and Horsa, and the royal families of the Northern lands. Still another version relates that *Odhin and Frigga had seven sons*, who founded the Anglo-Saxon Heptarchy. Perhaps this is yet another example of a ruling monarch actually presenting a huge probability of them being female? Here, not one, but seven such monarchs established dynasties of great spiritual significance, taking them back to the seven '*Mothers*.'

Frigga was goddess of the atmosphere, or rather of the clouds, and as such was represented as wearing either snow-white or dark garments, according to temperament. As Queen of the gods She possessed all future knowledge via her numerous oracular gifts. Described as elegant, tall, beautiful, and crowned with heron plumes, symbol of silence or forgetfulness. Her pristine robes are secured by a golden girdle, from which hang various keys. This became the symbol of the *good woman*, the fabled housekeeper of whom she was patron. Within the clouds She would spin the mists of the seas and of the skies, of all colours and variance in mood. Her brilliant jeweled distaff blazed across the night sky, recognized by many today as Orion's Girdle. Frigga was the goddess of conjugal and motherly love. But her vanity subjected even her to the laws of karma and all causality, for even the gods are subject to fate.

"My lily tall, from her saddle bearing,
I led then forth through the temple, faring
To th' altar-circle where, priests among,
Lofn's vows she took with unfalt'ring tongue."

VIKING TALES OF THE NORTH (R. B. Anderson)

Vjofn's duty was to incline obdurate hearts to love, to maintain peace and concord among mankind, and to reconcile quarrelling husbands and wives.

Lofn : Mild and gracious maiden Lofn (praise or love), whose duty it was to remove all obstacles from the path of lovers.

Syn (truth) guarded the door of Frigga's palace, refusing entrance to those forbidden without appeal. She presided over tribunals and trials. Where a *thing* was to be vetoed it was declared that *Syn* was against it.

Vara heard all oaths and punished perjurers, but rewarded those who faithfully kept their word.

Vör (faith) foresaw all occurrences.

Snort (virtue) mastered all study.

In southern Germany, other goddesses shared all of *Frigga's* unmistakable attributes. Her most common epithets were *Frau Holle, Hulda/Holda.* Legends abound of Her bountiful gifts to humankind, these being the distaff and the art of spinning, especially of flax. A proud housekeeper and stoic taskmistress. She gave short thrift to those She deemed lazy, yet rewarded the diligent with abundance.

Stone altars dedicated to the Lady of the Hearth, that is to say, *Bertha* and her popular variant, Pertcha, who is more widely revered as *The White Lady* have been discovered in areas of Germany distinct from those where Frigga and Holda carry that mantle. In Thuringia, She claimed the mythical mountain named Venusburg as Her retreat, wherein salubrious tales extoll Her sensual nature. But from within Her hollow cave, She silently observes the machinations of mankind even as She absorbs herself in care of Her plants and wards. These golden days of summer's past are said to be the glory when Bertha spun the world into being, an act for which She gained an enlarged, flat foot, pressed so long at the treadle. In mediaeval art she acquired the fond epithet: *la reine pédauque*. Again, it is beyond coincidence that yet another Teutonic goddess also spins the very fabric of the universe, the clouds, even Wyrd? Perhaps.

In Mecklenburg She adopts the title of Frau Gode/Wode (said to be the female form of Wotan/Votan) bringing gifts and awarding great prosperity upon all deserving souls She encounters while flying forth during Her yearly ride out from the hollow hill to lead the wild hunt mounted upon

Her white charger attended by Her cackling geese that squawk like baying hounds.

Across the more northerly regions of Germany, Her main form was Nerthus, simply the earth (also forms of Bertha and Pertcha). It is noteworthy to emphasize the similarity to Urdhr and Urth. Honour was paid to Her as a seemingly empty cart escorted by a priest chosen by lot for this particular honour circumambulated tribal boundaries. As She moved slowly towards Her lakeside sanctuary, all whose path She crossed were obliged to cease their tasks and pay homage, whether it be war or toil. The priest and cart would then slowly submerge into the beckoning waters. A cognate Scandinavian goddess was named Huldra.

Freyja, wife of Odr, is another Venusian goddess very much renowned for Her affairs of love and of death. Akin to the Nine forms of the Muse, Freyja assumes no less than *nine* titles or forms, but could it not be a further eight in addition to Her own. One aspect neatly fits each Compass point particularly as each relates to the major Valkyrie/Disir of the major Clan families those points represent.

Not all of these have been so easy to decipher, especially with regard to their etymological roots. Some of these names have posed etymological problems for scholars, while others are more straightforward to translate.

Both Freyja and Frigga share a nebulous existence beyond their native lands, so a cognate identity is problematic, but has merit. Reliable source material is scarce, but what there is confirms Her association with the Valkyrie!

Her nine prominent names possibly relate to the nine worlds of the World Tree. Three x three = Nine (realms), three for each level of the tree= Nine Muses. Nine nobles' virtues/worthies associated with knighthood and kingship through the honour of medieval courtly love.

The Nine Worthies

Nine historical, scriptural and legendary personifications of the Chivalric Ideal hold collectively the nine cognate virtues of soldierly courage and general-ship that originated during the early fourteenth century. Later connections with the genre of *Romance* literature divided them into three sets of three. Each man was considered an exemplary paragon of chivalry within his respective cultural tradition representing all facets of the perfect warrior and/or hero. Yet all were born of neither sovereign nor knighted gentry, having expressed such virtue by which they were later defined in a pre-heraldic era.

Glory and honour they acclaimed for their *Peoples* in possessing great proficiency in matters of war and compassion, mercy and justice in matters of peace. There is a 13th century German ecclesiastical frieze entitled, *Neun Gute Helden* which is the earliest known representation of the Nine Worthies.

Describing this from left to right: the three Christians, Charlemagne bearing an eagle upon his shield, King Arthur displaying three crowns and Godfrey of Bouillon with a dog laying before him.

Next, the three pagans, Julius Caesar, Hector and Alexander the Great bearing a griffon upon his shield, and finally, the three Jews, David holding a scepter, Joshua and Judas Maccabeus.

All Nine are said to embody the *genius* of a particular ideal associated with the Perfect Knight. And, though each remains an individual, they all retain a singular universal and eternal precedent. They became a popular theme within the masked balls of that chivalric period in History.

By the late fourteenth century, Lady Worthies began to complement the Nine Worthies, accompanying them everywhere. Later still, nine of the *Most Illustrious Ladies of All Ages and Nations* chosen from history, legend and scripture were placed along side their masculine foils, albeit the lists varied extensively.

What these lists suggest quite pertinently, is a growing association with complementary pairs of masculine and feminine qualities, a harmonic virtue and a grand design acquiring three levels of society, both mystically and in secular life. We have yet another clear example of the warrior, the priest and the provider.

Chapter Seven

VALKYRIES

Poetic terms for Valkyries find expression through definition of arms.[xlii] These are used when referring to weapons and armour, particularly as death maidens. They wield shields and spears generally, though swords and bows are not unknown. Eight Skalds are able to recite impressive lists and genealogies linked to all names both Freyja and Odhin are known by, including those within their train of Valkyries. Odhin possessed numerous other consorts, wives and maids from within this familiar class of spirits that are better known to us by their role as Valkyrie.

These include: ***Hildr,*** *Göndul, Hlökk, Mist,* ***Skögul.*** Occasionally this may also include: *Hrund, Eir, Hrist, and* ***Skulde,*** *totaling Nine.* They are called *Norns who shape necessity.*

Valkyries in the shape of ravens or swans have often chosen mortal lovers to ease their loneliness as they wander across the land. Some manuscripts[xliii] contain an extended list of Valkyrie names covering all variants of 24 to 29 . In the Prose Edda, the *Gylfaginning* affords them deific status, where they are named as *ale maids* who serve the *ale* to those rejoicing in the Halls.

This is a serious underestimation borne of possible misunderstanding regarding the import of the subtle qualities and virtue of *alu* veiled in metaphoric expression given here as *mead/soma* - the poetic inspiration by which all names noted in the songs and stories are granted immortality in the *Halls of the Gods.* Looking more deeply into this, we see the trace pattern emerging of the Houzle, the emphasis of the troth, of sumbel, its consumption as a dedicatory rite between and within a Clan family to protect each other.

The presence of the Muse within the words that express the inspiring *thought* and within the *memory* of the skald reciting them may be unequivocally given parallel in Huggin and Muggin, the two/twin and foremost Valkyrie. It is not beyond ease that these plus seven others from the Compass round suggestive of the nine muses gracing the fields of Apollo. We have the mead as the inspiring soma of eternal memory – the qualities of the *inspirit / egregore*, the sentient ancestral mind, evinced though the culminatory mechanics of the Houzle. Within this *Cup of Death* is either an overflowing of mead, symbolic of *virtue* gifted by the relevant Valkyrie assigned to that family, or an emptiness that denotes the absence of virtue.

Hence *girt terror and fearful dread.*

To be without such protection, devoid of providence is a living death: an unfavourable Fate indeed. Roy Bowers placed enormous stress upon the vitality of the spear and cauldron as an act of supreme grace; by the drawing of its wood into the steaming metal cauldron, some measure of benign fate is achieved, visible in the moisture upon its tip.

The spear and cauldron rite within the Clan mythos express the union of heaven and earth through the striking of the spear [as the force of time] into the seething cauldron [of all potential, from within the absu/void of Fate]. The spear [as the fourth nail] enters this void, drawing down the mystic fire, the *magnetic tide of the moon*, earthing it within the waters of eternity.

Briefly, *'time stops and fate is overcome.* As the spear is withdrawn from the cauldron, time is drawn from eternity; precious drops of divine inspiration and essence drip from its tip, for which we partake as *Houzel*– the aqua vitae of the black sun, our communion with the gods. Wisdom is released through Love, the emotive anchor of the lunar kalas.

It is the point where '*midnight* [black sun/cauldron] *meets the evening star'* [moon].

This is the true meaning of *'Drawing down the Moon.'*

The Pale Leukathea is the multi-faceted jewel, of whom we see only one facet. The mirror of Venus beams down her subtle influences, Her radiant magics of flux and stasis. Roy Bowers refers to "woman as the lesser moon" because the tides of her body are in sync with that great silver orb in the heavens, and by which, in like fashion she generates, nurtures and controls creativity, intuition, emotion and all things of the "unconscious state."

She is thus the presiding genius behind all creation, life and death. As Shakti, she is Mistress [and compliment] to the male mysteries.

Another stanza refers to them as those who *choose the slain* and to whom they will grant victory. This substantiates them as having strong links to those invoked over their shields when commencing battle. References to Valkyries appear throughout other verses that describe such events:

"There I perceive Valkyries and ravens,
accompanying the wise victory-tree [Odhin]
to the drink of the holy offering [Baldr's funeral feast]
Within have appeared these motifs. "

The Old English terms – *wælcyrge* and *wælcyrie* appear with considerable repetition in OE Ms and the recorders of such literature considered this term to mean human sorceresses and also certain goddesses becoming subject to negative glossing by religious zealots. [xliv]

Female figures as cup and horn-bearers.

Silver figures were popular as burial charms. One portrays a female figure facing forward, a figure upon a horse, facing yet another figure with a shield. A female figure bears a horn to a rider on an eight-legged horse. This brings to mind the vital deed in Beowulf set in Hrothgar's Mead Hall, where his Queen carried forth the drinking horn as an act of providence, the performing act of grace amongst brethren, kith and kin. Many Valkyrie names carry associations with the elements of battle, in particular the spear, even so, their florid attributes are perhaps given to excessive flowing by skalds reciting their tales for effect among the halls of their hosts. Some names have clear connections to Orlog, Fate and Wyrd. (Sources for Valkyrie Names) [xlv]

Two Incantations survive from Meresburg. One in particular describes the Idisi as binding and befuddling an enemy army. As the Disir, these female *family* guardians share considerable similarities with the Norse Valkyrie. The incantation reads:

"I Once the Idisi sat, sat here and there, some bound fetters, some hampered the army, some untied fetters"

These autonomous matriarchs share their numerous skills through inspiration within crafts, arts and wisdom to those mortals they favour. Yet, in spite of certain similarities, the disir and the Valkyrie are as different as Irminsul and Yggdrassil; both fulfill significantly divergent cultural eschatologies. Primarily, only the *dís may also be a Norn.* The Norns pronounce the *fatum* [fate] of others, weaving all within their web of Wyrd. Sometimes they traverse the land, but in ethereal form, not upon horses or any other beast.

Heroic poetry escalated the legends attributed to these shield maidens and ancestral mothers, who continue to protect their own in death – to carry them safely to the halls of the gods. Later, they even acquired the ability to engage with mortals. Others relate an interesting association with the activities of the Norns who determine the lot and length of each soul from initial inspiration to final expiration.

Elements culled from the seidr women also find their way into conflation with these magical female forms. Myths of debts due to both Odhin and his beautiful wife Freyja concern Her as the *one who chooses* the souls of the slain asserting Her appearance as a Valkyrie, though she bears no connection to the Norns.

Geiraskogul and/or Geiramul:

Skogul= wind [shaker -Guilvig?] and high towering [spinning] castle, and also shield. [Memory]

Geiramul = spear. [Thought] The only Valkyrie mentioned in the Voluspa to bring the fallen to Odhin.

As Odhin's messengers and warriors, these very much suggest his spear and shield; similarly as such they would represent, thought and memory as both ravens and wolves. This primal twin forms our Clan's protectress and shield maiden of Truth! Her name, composed of 8 letters for the stations of the Compass is equally formed from the four vowels within it, one for each cardinal point:

Jotunheimhr =Air
Muspelheimhr = Fire
Vanaheimhr = Water
Niflheimhr = Ice
[but would work very well with Alfheimhr (earth) as the sacred mound]

Chapter Eight

FRAU GAUD: THE ORDER OF 1734

Born from within The Multi-Faceted Creatrix the enigmatic force of the Pale Faced Goddess much revered by The Clan of Tubal Cain becomes accessible in Her main form as emergent Truth. From that perspective we discover another facet in the form of *Frau Gaud, Mistress of the Wild Hunt* whose origin hails from the Thuringian regions of the mythical lands of Thule, the central focus of the Clan's Mythos.

Looking at a demographic we can discern the spatial ratios quite visibly. A pattern of popularity and familiarity between and for the major Teutonic goddess forms emerges conclusively. With regard to the wild hunt especially, the central regions of Germania pinpoint Holle and Pertcha very closely in regional appearance and number; Frau Gode and Herke appear further north and are again fairly even by comparison with each other though of significantly diminished popularity to those more frequent and common toponyms found in the central regions. The order then is as follows, in increasing number: Gode, Herke, Holle and Pertcha. Curiously, despite Frigga/Frikka being the best known in modern times, she was the least familiar and popular before conversion to Christianity. This parallels the rise in popularity of Isis by the Romans, where she had previously been held by Egyptians in much lesser regard.[xlvi]

Nerthus has finally been acknowledged by modern students of Northern beliefs and culture as the named goddess lauded within a good proportion of Germanic religious practices around the 1st century CE. Central to the Heiros Gamos, Her role became the Mistress of all fecundity assigned to the welfare of Her people, being almost identical to the worship and beliefs of the Scandinavians since the Bronze Age. A conclusion may then be assumed of their compatibility and mutual source. [xlvii]

Seven ancient Tribes make up the nucleus of the tenacious barbarians of whom Tacitus writes:

"The Langobardi are distinguished by being few in number. There is nothing especially noteworthy about these states individually, but they are distinguished by a common worship of Nerthus, that is, Mother Earth, and believe she intervenes in human affairs and rides through their peoples. There is a sacred grove on an island of the Ocean, in which there is a consecrated chariot draped with a cloth, which the priest alone may touch. He perceives the presence of the goddess in the innermost shrine and with great reverence escorts her in her chariot, which is drawn by female cattle. There are days of rejoicing then and the countryside celebrates the festival, wherever she deigns to visit and to accept hospitality. No one goes to war, no one takes up arms. All objects of iron [i.e. weapons] are locked away then and only then do they exercise peace and quiet, only then do they prize them, until the goddess has had her fill of society, and the priest brings her back to the temple. Afterwards the chariot, the cloth, and if one may believe it, the deity herself are washed in a hidden lake. Hence arises dread of the mysterious, and piety, which keeps them ignorant of what only those who are about to perish may see."[xlviii]

Clearly this Goddess deemed the *Mother of All* is held in awe equal to Her reverence. The name Nerthus has other linguistically disputed forms such as *Nertus and Nerthum*. Some scholars assert that Nerthus is a masculine *form* and incorrect in its usage for a Goddess. It has also been suggested by some that Nerthus properly refers to the Male deity of a Terra Mater, or goddess of the earth whom Nerthus accompanies, but this view remains unsupported by the qualities and potencies these forms possess and control.[xlix]

"A divinity in a wagon is well known in Germanic lore, thus there is little need to speculate that Tacitus borrowed the idea from Roman sources. According to the Prose Edda, Thor drives a wagon drawn by goats, Frey arrives at Baldr's funeral in a cart led by a boar, and Freyja rides in a car pulled by cats. Njörd too is known as god of wagons in a skaldic verse cited in the primary manuscript of Snorri's Edda; where other manuscripts have Vana guð (god of the Vanir), Codex Regius has vagna guð (god of the wagon). The Big Dipper (Ursa Major) was commonly known as the Wain,

or wagon. In skaldic poetry, Odhin is known as runni vagna, mover of wagons; vinr vagna, friend of wagons; vári vagna, protector of wagons; and valdr vagnbrautar, ruler of the wagon-road. The sky itself, home of the gods; is known as the land of wagons (land vagna); indicating that the constellations were imagined as the gods circling the heavens in their car.[l]*"*

Other variants of the fabled cart, describe a veiled Idol, more probably of Freyja, though these seem to better reflect the winter games and frolics that imitate forthcoming spring union of the fecundating polarities of all life. Many such celebrations brightened the darkest Yuletides in the bleak latitudes of those lands of fire and ice of the unforgiving North. In the following statement; the gem of truth gleams forth in the personage of Njordr whose etymological cognate - Ordhr/Urdhr bridges the dearth of comprehension so common of an often blinkered academia, finding here some measure of affirmation in the synthesis and shift of and between genders. What is most fascinating in drawing together this example is that both Njordr and Urdhr represent various aspects and qualities of 'Time,' which are elaborated upon within the conclusion.

"It has long been recognized that the name Nerthus is an etymon of Njörðr, a Vanir god, and father of Freyr and Freyja. Grimm himself noted that the name Nerthus was identical to the later Old Norse name Njörðr, an "identity as obvious as that of Freyr to Freyja."[li] Much has been made of this apparent gender gap. Over the years, scholars have sometimes assumed that the deity always had been male or had changed gender reflecting the reduction in the status of women, between the times of Tacitus and Saxo.[lii]

Why these foundations are so important to our understanding of the Clan's Mythos will slowly become evident as the legacy of belief, scattered among the English peoples, preserved in our cultural heritage, in folk lore, belief and magics, are now explored to their celebrated conclusion. Other more idiosyncratic aspects of the divine nature find manifestation though such cultural identities as *Goden* [aka *Woden/Votan*] and his Lady, *Frau Goden*, who exalt the virtue of a complementary yet essential mirror a unified absolute in the divine exemplified in the popular Hindu forms of *Shiva and Shakti.* Each assumed prominence and favour according to era, subject as they are to the politics of religion and culture.

In particular, this coupling originated in the mountainous regions of Germania given to the later traditions of *Frau Holle, Perchta and Bertcha* where the great track ways of the ancients, the causeways of the gods, hewn from the earth by the legendary hooves of Baldr's Horse, serve as the route of the wanderers in their quest to return to that Source and progenitor of our being. From Jacob Grimm we learn of the sacred locations deemed coterminous with the Holy Omphalos and the sacred groves therein.[liii]

Folk magics abound with acts of sympathetic cures and charms, casting bond first betwixt *Odhin* and Baldr as Master's of the Horse, with all riders and Horsemen, a fascinating tangent, I hope to explore some other time. Certain Calendrical nodes have been designated auspicious for such cures; St Stephens Day remains a primary example.[liv] Suffice to say here at this time there is a wealth of lore weaving the more recent folklore of English tradition with the myths and beliefs of the Northern Peoples of the early centuries. Baldr typifies the brave, bold and beautiful, the perfect warrior whose boasts are not made in idle jest. His protection is a divine gift, yet one that carries the seed of his destruction, for his boast invites the instrument of his death. Thus slain he becomes the seed of himself reborn as Váli, his heroic brother, upon the feast day of St Stephens, as one dies, the dawn births his counterpart, as Castor and Pollux and all tanists duos of like.

Winter Solstice marks the (literal) advent of Lux, of light. A full Moon at this time affirms the conjunctive Contract of cyclical renewal aligned to the stars in the heavens above. The Day after Solstice Night, or Yule, the wren and robin exchange their spirit, one to the other in continuum of this ancient tale. St. Stephen is the patron of Horsemen, Baldr the bright sun, and sacrificial king reborn to his waxing twin, the *Jul bukk*, or *Bukker,* the festive goat of Thor, the gift giver throughout the Northern lands in Winter, horned master and beast of Initiation to whom oaths of the horsemen are offered during the winter months. The winter spirit of the *Bukka* then is no random troll, but is no less than the totem vehicle of the bondsmen of all warriors, Thor, the smith, the wielder of Mjolnir, the Hammer of the Law and scales of justice. [lv]

Winter games and festivities still involve significant traces of these warrior traits of valour and skill most finding expression within the festive arts of the sword rappers and dancers, shadowed by the not insignificant presence of the *obby oss* and other localized totemic beasts that die and are happily resurrected within traditional mummers plays. A renewal of all solar gods [os the Anglo Saxon term for god] is linked to the re-birth of the Sun at the winter solstice. Hence the White horse, Sleipnir leads the hunt out from the Mound at Candlemas.

In the Summer, the Solstice denotes the changeover to the waning cycle at the *Feast of St. John* the occasion of Mary's transience.

Chapter Nine

THULE AS THE MYTHICAL CASTLE WITHIN THE CLAN TODAY

Looking at medieval maps of northern Europe, we may easily plot the four towns listed by Roy Bowers in his Basic Structure of the Craft as the mounds hosting the indwelling virtue of the cardinal winds via their cognate towns – Tettens, Luci, Carenos and Nod. In the centre of this cross lies, unsurprisingly, Thuringia, the fundamental origin to Rose Beyond the Grave.

The poetic beauty of this place has been so maligned by association with the political machinations of the last century. Therefore, we must distance our understanding and use of this once mystical land to one that had no part in its early histories.

We must restore Edin to the rightful place within the Clan Cosmology where the idealisms of a magical eschatology founded in myth and legends of a Medieval Europe thrive again. Complex mysteries shared by John [Jones], based on his own knowledge and experience of the Castle and the Rose, the Mound and the Maze, the Five Rings and the Clan Mythos and by Roy Bowers (whose own insightful gifts synthesized a manifest formulae of them) have together provided us with the means to now accomplish that vision. May we reclaim anew our multi-layered cultural and craft heritage through these archaic and mystical resonances which reside at the very heart of our root psyche. Edin exists wherever the Stang, as Irminsul is erected.

Everything we engage is enabled through the memory of experience, the Mind articulates through myriad visions in order to choose a single image that best expresses the impressions analysed through a conjunction of psychic and emotive reaction in tandem with the visual registry perceived in or out of true context. Perennial philosophy condenses these principles into rhetorical abstracts through engagement of the higher mind, bypassing the realm of what is perceived as real to the ideal within all things. Our aim then is to that which it knows as The Real, the single Truth that permeates All things. In this we at once realize the vast gulf that yawns between the world of our forefathers and our own, and yet in understanding the nature of memory we may yet bridge that abyss, the seeming void of contradiction and lack. Therefore, all events become de-mystified, de-mythologized as we allow ourselves ingress within a world distinct only in its superficialities. We remain connected to the experiences that gripped the fears and fantasies of our ancestors as we engage the Virtue proper. This is its primary function, en-souling the Compass as the Merkabah, the vehicle of congress across time.

"Ritual is an obsessive repetitive activity--often a symbolic dramatization of the fundamental needs of the society, whether economic, biological, social, or sexual. Mythology is the rationalization of these same needs, whether they are all expressed in overt ceremonial or not' (1942: 78). Social and legal structure, for example, seems to derive from the same structural 'needs'. The extensive work of Georges Dumezil and his followers on the relationship of Indo-European myth and the culture's probable tripartite social structure bears this out. The same basis underlies the art and literature of a culture; indeed, this underlying conceptual structure should in for many cultural artifact, any construct that has a dimension beyond the merely useful or ordinary: 'Myth, art, religion, and language are all symbolic expressions of the creative spirit in man; in them this spirit takes on objective, perceptible form, becoming conscious of itself through man's consciousness of it"

(Neumann 1964:369)

The Five Rings and Ultima Thule

The five rings are in fact the real treasure, the very real mystery of the Clan pertaining to Roy Bowers 'Round of Life.' In fact, it is the very heart of the Compass relating to the Male, Female and Priestly Mysteries and the rites and locations wherein each are experienced. To fully understand its context, we need to return to the legendary land of Thule.

Returning briefly to the historical description of Ultima Thule as a shifting place that is by day and night continually turning that is no place known and unbound by time. It is composed without proper land nor sea nor air, but a sort of mixture of all three of the consistency of a jellyfish in which one can neither walk nor sail of three elements, of earth, water and air, no fire (again the very elements employed within idiosyncratic descriptives by Bowers and Jones within their literary legacies); this can be seen as no less than the gift of Prometheus, literally and metaphorically. These three elements combine together within the mythical land of Thule referred to emphatically by both men as the castle that spins upon three elements. Bowers heralds the NE area of the compass as 'the Goddess comes from here'; this would of course on any map place it geographically within Thuringia!

The triadic Creatrix alluded to by Bowers and Jones as Hekate in a letter to Norman Gills (with the caveat that She is a mere approximation) is more fittingly – revealed as The Fates/Norns who filter their Virtue through the three main female deities of the northern peoples: Nerthus/Freyja/Holda. But through whom these find further expression and significance, is slowly unfurling.

Etymology of god:

The English word "god" as derived from the Proto-Germanic **g**uđan is found in the 6th century Christian Codex Argenteus, and is generally accepted as the earliest written Germanic root form. Though a reconstructed Proto-Indo-European form ǵhu-tó-m based on the root ǵhau (ə) [lvi] meaning 'to call' or invoke, it has tremendous implications regarding the more mystical elements of our own spiritual praxis. It is the animate force or Virtue within all things, yet sourced beyond them.

Etymology of Gar:

Gar: (O.E.) gar spear, (from P.Gmc. gaizo- cf. O.N. geirr, O.S., O.H.G. ger. *Ger* spear: from PIE ghaiso- stick, spear) also stang is Germanic for staff! (see goad: gad point, spearhead, and arrowhead; from P.Gmc. gaido cf. Lombardic *gaida* spear; from PIE *ghei-* Gk. khaios shepherd's staff; O.E. gar spear; O.Ir. gae spear). *gungnir*. Gar: gift –spear: is also the name of ᚸ, a rune of the late Anglo-Saxon futhorc. Phonetically, *gar* represents the /g/ sound. It is a modification of the plain *gyfu* rune.

These definitions tighten the correlation between the staff/stang/tree and indwelling deity, perceived as Virtue, the ancestral egregore. Hence it becomes the focus during all rites. It describes the mound by its presence as the axis mundi and anima mundi, as Ida and Pingala, the twin serpents of the caduceus upon the tree relating to all things of heritage, oracular wisdoms, magics, devotions and celebrations pertinent to their natures.

Skáldskaparmál has more information regarding the spear and how Loki obtained it by nefarious means. It had been fashioned by the dwarfs known as the *Sons of Ivaldi* under the mastery of the blacksmith dwarf Dvalin. The spear is described as having the ability to be unrelenting in aim and intent, and deadly efficient in action as it pierces cleanly its target. Its purpose as the 'Spear of Destiny' will also become more apparent as we move through all modalities that add succour and support to our mythos. Runes: The early futhorc was identical to the Elder Futhark except for the split of ᚨ ain to three variants ᚪ āc, ᚫ æsc and ᚩ ōs, resulting in 26 runes. In England the Northumbrian futhorc further extended to 28 and finally to 33 runes. Due to Anglo-Saxon Christianization in the 7th century, the futhorc gradually became replaced with the Latin alphabet by around the end of the 9th century.

For three hundred more years, substitution for a word by a rune occurred with decreasing regularity until the runes disappeared from common usage. The first 24 of these directly continue the Elder Futhark letters, extended by five additional runes representing vowels and extended vowels (á, æ, ý, ia, ea) as exponded by E.J. Jones, used by him exclusively in the Mill Chant – that which binds us back to the Source, uniting the spark within to that greater spark without. All is one and all alone and ever more shall be so!

These holy vowels form the five runic chants distinct to our tradition for the sighting of the boundaries cross points and centre (five for the symbols at your door) TH and W were introduced into written Latin to represent [**θ**] and [w], but were eventually replaced with th and w.[lvii] Breaking down the word Th-ur-ing-ia, we are able to compose a specific meaning relevant to the [ur] archaic land of the ancestors, the followers dedicated to the sacred enclosure of, Ing! [land]

The rune letter for 'th' is ᚦ, meaning thorn. Intriguingly, it also prefixes Th-ule and Th-ing. Specifically, thorn means 'phallic' [as in Irminsul] but also a protected enclosure. Applied to Thule, it becomes the protected enclosure of the elements. Applied to Thing, it is the protected enclosure, the meeting place dedicated to Ing. Applied to Thuringia, it is the protected ancestral space dedicated to Ing!

Given that Irminsul is the great pillar or pole, [axis mundi], it becomes the bridge that links Thuringia at the base, to Thing at the centre and to Thule at the tip; we have instantly the nine worlds glyph and a symbol represented by the three nails.

'The Order of the Sun'

Thule – egress, the place of desire [eternal bliss]

Thing – congress, the place of meeting [castle and all realms]

Thuringia – ingress – the place of origin [access point in ritual]

Illustrated by the 'Serpent Stang' with mounted arrows crossed upon the pole, we may consider that the word for pole in Scandinavian countries is actually 'Stang'; this glyph encapsulates the entire Cosmology of the Clan Mythos, of the nine worlds of the three realms. Importantly, it indicates the space in which we begin all work, the 'Thing' at the centre of the stang, in Midgardhr, in the ring of stones in the circle round. From this great enclosure beneath the sacred oak, the 'gardh' tree itself, we traverse via the compass the upper and lower realms, to the castle and all realms. We ascend upwards to Asgardhr [Thule] or descend below to Utgardhr, the ancestral mound/Thuringia.

Anglo-Saxon Runes.

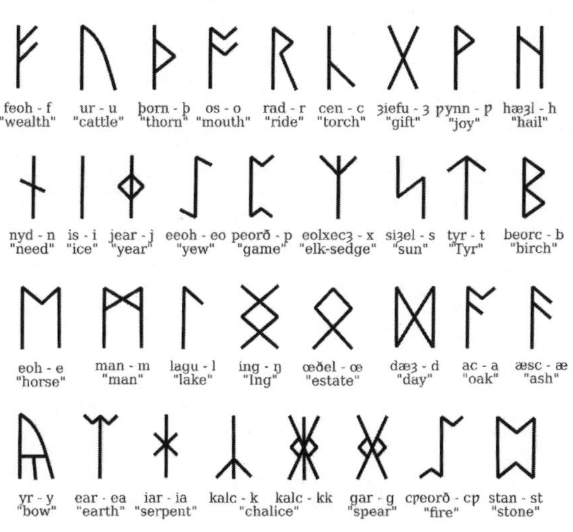

They are very similar to those also known as 'Frisian' with minor differences. They also include the elongated vowels [five] used by Roy Bowers and E.J. Jones (as above) for the calls at the solar cross and centre points of the compass to summon the winds.

These are the five vowels used in our chants and have two recensions, one male and one female, generating two opposing swastikas, the archaic symbol for movement. These runes also include elemental additions, not present in the older Futhark.

Chapter Ten

THE SPINDLE

Essential to the weaving art, the spindle is recognizable as an historical emblem of security. In an 8th century BCE inscription at Karatepe we discover

"In those places which were formerly feared, where a man fears... to go on the road, in my days even women walked with spindles"

Female divinity in hoary patronage of spinners has been the focus of many myths and countless legends providing the basis by which it became established as a feminine, magical art. Adam and Eve clothed themselves in Eden after her industry and innovative talents to spin and weave the thread to cover their bodies. For thousands of years since that time, others too have been named as Mistress of the Distaff from Neith to Isis, Bridget to Mary, Athene to Minerva, Venus to Saule and Frigga to Freyja, as the spinners and weavers of the stars, the clouds, words and even the fabric of time itself. A legend in Scandinavia concerns the star constellation Orion and the Girdle of stars named *Friggjar rockr, Frigga*'s distaff. Friday (Frigga's day) is held sacred to all spinners, and in honour of her, no distaff, or spindle must turn.

The concept of weaving even relates to the mechanics of mythology where we discover that the English word *text* is derived from the Latin word for weaving, *texare*, providing a plausible source for the terms used in the expression of myth. For example: *weaving a story*. For the Norse peoples, Frigga is a goddess associated with weaving. The Scandinavian *Song of the Spear* quoted in Njals Saga, offers a valuable description of Valkyries as weavers upon a loom. Holda taught the secret of making linen from flax. The *Kalevala*, a Finnish epic, references several spinning and weaving goddesses. Superstition regards spinning as the handiwork of the devil, the craft of attraction by enchantment and incantation, of woven charms for dubious intent. Frau Holda, in spinning the etheric bridge between all worlds, offers yet another fascinating clue towards the discovery of who these goddesses, named for their regional preference, really represent.

How easily these tools became allied with Fate, used by the Norns, the Parcae and the Moirae, all triads in fact. An exception occurs in Lithuanian Myth, where seven goddesses share the work, although the latter do not measure the thread of life; this is left to *chance*, better known as Providence. Historically, femininity and spinning were synonymous; as were the enchantments they ensue. Until the major wars of the 20th century, an unmarried daughter of any household held the position of *spinster* in order to earn her keep. So symbolic is this function of women in culture, tales across Europe immortalize the trials of men disguised as woman, or women disguised as men, where knowledge of the spinning craft has revealed their true sex. [lviii]

Rhea is said to have shared her arte of spinning with Zeus and even Idunna is an exemplary mistress of this arcane skill. Centuries before the popularity of the newly emerging Isis, Neith was always the goddess of weaving. She was known as the most ancient one, to whom the other gods turned for wisdom. Identifiable by her emblem, the loom's shuttle, worn crown-like upon her head. Neith, though a fine spinner and weaver, was held in awe as the most archaic and complex example of a powerful and aggressive warrior-hunter of Sais [House of thc Bee], her skills were unmatchable by mortal man.

Named 'Mistress of the Bow' her emblem was composed of a shield and crossed bows (sometimes arrows) mounted on a pole. Famed for her wisdom, Neith would be asked *to judge* or arbitrate between the feuding deities. Using purely the symbol of the rune, Neith would equate with *Urdhr (Yr)*. Neith watched over the dead, even providing their funerary wrappings. As the goddess of weaving, her symbolic glyph quickly became the loom, labeling her as the universal mother of the cosmos, of Ra, Apophis and benefactress of humankind. She was the 'great cow' or 'great flood.' These epithets place her beside other deities of creation and of death, especially within the Vedic, Norse and Teutonic cultures. The staff/stang is equally the spindle and distaff, the spear and bow; all attributes of the rune Yr – the (gardhr) tree!

It is also said that *Neith is both feminine and masculine– 'two thirds masculine, one third feminine,'* (Esna, vol. 5, p. 110) – both mother and father, "who inaugurated birth when birth had not yet been, having "appeared from herself," (Esna, vol. 5, p. 253).

Invocations and prayers hail Her as She who separated all things from their opposite state, as light, life, land and time. Her gigantic loom of the heavens spins out the eternity of all things, and all things are under Her aegis. Neith served best the Pharaoh in her provision of Linen and anointing oil. The inference is of protection, known as The Cloak of Night by- EJJ & RB. Yet, despite knowing Her protective role through Her symbol of the crossed arrows upon the Stang, I was un-prepared for the enormity of Her significance, both as an arcane force and qualitative goddess.

In Greco-Roman Myth, three maidenly sisters named the Hesperides together with a Serpent were given the task of guarding the tree of golden apples of Hera, Queen and mother of the gods; tasting of honey, these apples imbue vigour and vitality. Idunna shares much of this mythos, laced with chthonic elements regarding Her golden apples of longevity, or rather eternal life, and are again significant in the benefactress role, yet more so concerning the darker element of taking charge of the spirit in death as much as in life.

Another beautiful Queen, visible in the night sky as Venus was regarded by Norse peoples is *Friggjarstjarna or Frigga's star.* Like Venus, Frigga had similar associations with marriage and childbirth. Lady's Bedstraw (Galium verum) as a sedative was named *Frigga's grass.*

Frigga, Odhin, Huggin, Munnin and other Valkyrie offer gifts to Hermóðr to enable their return to Asgardhr. Only two gifts are specifically mentioned: a white linen robe for Frigga and a golden ring for *Fulla* her attendant. Two more were named *Hlín, Gná.*

'*Odhin [Odhin] had two brothers. Ve, and Vili. These, his brothers, governed the realm when he was gone. Once, when Odhin stayed away so long that the Æsir thought he would never return, brothers began to divide his inheritance; but his wife Frigga they shared between them. However, a short while afterwards, Odhin returned and took possession of his wife again.*'

This revives the Arthurian declaration of sovereignty. Comparisons have been proposed regarding Frigga's role in this story to that of sacred queens during certain periods in ancient Egypt, when a king was king by virtue of being the queen's husband.

Frigga is, according to modern perceptions, the highest goddess of the *Aesir*, as Freyja is of the *Vanir*. Suggestions present sensible examples they are one and the same goddess. Certain similarities do exist between the two: both had flying cloaks of falcon feathers and engaged in shape-shifting; Frigga was married to Odhin while Freyja was married to Odr; both had necklaces of significance to their own mythos, were personified by Earth, assisted in matters of hearth, home, marriage and childbirth. Yet Freyja was unknown in southern Germany. In other areas knowledge of both names is confirmed, however, scant evidence supports the very real possibility of their being appreciated as the same goddess.

Yet another possibility exists in Frigga and Freyja being two of a distinct triad of goddesses; the third could be *Hnoss* or *Idunna*. If this proves more fruitful with further research, the best we may say at present is they work in an entirely different manner to other known triads. Perhaps if they also be viewed as regional names, titles given of local significance that refer to a more universal concept, we might be closer to understanding more than is immediately apparent?

Looking into the etymology of Frigga, Old Saxon Fri, and Old English Frigga, all are derived from Germanic - *Frijjō*. Frigga is also cognate with Sanskrit *prīyā́* which means wife. The root also appears in Old Saxon *Fri* which means *beloved lady* that in Icelandic as frjá means *to love*. This constellation is on the celestial equator, suggesting that all circumambulating stars rotating in the night sky may have associations with Frigga's spinning wheel.

Chapter Eleven

WYRD/FATE/ORLOG

Spinning is a craft considered to be one of the most potent gifts of the gods. Many goddesses including Namaah, Mary, Frigga and even Venus used their arte to weave the fortunes of those whom they favour from birth to death, marking all five stages [inclusive of youth, love, maturity]. All must first be wound upon a spindle from Her great [dis]staff. These beliefs are cognate with Greek and Norse mythology and also to much faerie lore, especially as the Godmothers who bring blessings to all newborn babies.

They have no realistic comparison, as even those fair ladies of fortune whose attributes have linked them by act or deed, are no more than pale facsimiles. In Roman Myth, the Fates were known as *Parcae* and sporadically as, *Fatae*. Even within Greek Mythology, the Fates were goddesses who oversaw the organization of society administering the appropriate action in response to imbalance or error -*sin*. Hesiod records in his Cosmogony of the Gods [Theogony] the origin of all things as Khaos, the formless void and disorder. As the instrument of divine order and law, Zeus succeeds in balancing those primal forces of the cosmos, destroying all potential threats against future equilibrium.

As we have discovered thus far, the three *Moirai/Parcae* or *Fatae*, plural of *fatum* meaning prophetic declaration, oracle, or destiny are daughters of Ananke [*necessity*] but also of the primeval goddess Nyx (Night), hence their later associations with Hekate and the Fates. [lix] The English words fate(native Wyrd) and faerie (magic, enchantment), are both derived from *fata, fatum*[lx] *Moira, aisa, moros* signifies *portion* or *part*. Another link is given through etymology [from *moira/aisa/moros*] to the muse,[lxi] and by that *virtue* to all things of the mind and memory.

By extension *Moira* is the portion in glory, happiness and the inevitability of death as we all hurtle towards our ultimate destiny through all those events whether expected or not. In the arcane world, it was believed by many that their *lot* in life was pre-destined, that is according to lineage and heritage, or class/caste etc.

Moira was above even the Olympian gods, where even Zeus fell under Her edict in the rightful *order of things.*[lxii]This notion of looking forwards albeit retrospectively, was how they foresaw the consequential karmic patterns, weaving all together within a future destined to be, yet which could be engaged and influenced by the meritous past. Three aetheric forms spun the words for the skalds to sing, so that all things would be recorded and never forgotten. In this knowledge lay the seed potential for nurturing the vine of self-will; if just and honourable, it secured the thread of remembrance and the reward of a *better fate.*

The Moirai were commonly described as old women as severe as they were ugly, with fearful deformities and were commonly assigned to several chthonic goddesses, all of whom were again said to *direct fate according to necessity.* [lxiii]

- Clotho carries a *spindle* or a roll (codex Fatae).
- Lachesis carries a *staff,* often pointed at the stars and luminaries.
- Atropos (Aisa) carries a pair of *scales,* and or shears/scissors along with a scroll, a wax tablet or a sundial. All three have also been depicted with staffs or scepters and occasionally even with *Crowns,* symbols of ruler-ship and dominion.

Aphrodite (Venus) possibly because of her quite early titanic existence was revered as Aphrodite-Urania the 'eldest of all Fates.' At some point, it is clear that a patriarchal coup was visited upon the arcane status of that baneful Triad.[lxiv] Perpetuated *ad nasueum* ever since, it remains vital that the full extent of consequence Patriarchy is held accountable, being the first to systematically diminish *She* from *Asherah* demeaning her to an unknown and almost non-existent, almost irrelevant consort [if and where mentioned at all].

Zeus acquired the virtue of so many divine ladies from his sexual conquests, not least of whom, Themis from whom Zeus subsumed her office of Law and Order. In legend, they fused the Moirae' said to hold and to dispense this virtue.[lxv]

"A supposed epithet Zeus Moiragetes, meaning "Zeus Leader of the Moirai" was inferred by Pausanias from an inscription he saw in the 2nd century CE at Olympia: "As you go to the starting-point for the chariot-race there is an altar with an inscription to the 'Bringer of Fate.' This is plainly a surname of Zeus, who knows the affairs of men all that the Fates give them and all that is not destined for them."[lxvi]

Germanic Matres, Matrones and several other female deities formed commonly in threes, parallel and even suggest quite strongly the Norns and also the Valkyries. It becomes readily apparent that Anglo-Saxon Wyrd is indistinct from the Norse Urdhr; both concepts of fate are rooted in *wert* to turn/ wind bearing strong connections to *spindle and distaff.* Further north and east, other goddesses indicate the same principles, exercising the same autonomy above the gods and who are portrayed as benefactresses to humankind. These include the Hindu deity Lakshmi, who is linked to Clan Mythos through the potency and allegiance to and of - OD.[lxvii]

Within the 'Prose Eddas' referenced as three mysterious beings, they are - *High-One, Just-as-High, and Third.*' Originally, the Norns recorded such deeds upon wooden staves, carved in runic form, yet through later influences from contemporary Graeco-Roman cognates, the Moirai began to assume the activities of spinners and weavers. Odhin's own hermetic quest to gather for himself all knowledge that this may be preserved among all good men as the mysteries began within this Arcane triad. Thus Man and god feasted together within the Halls of Asgardhr, assembled daily to hear the affectations of the world, to learn of its woes and settle them there, in the sacred enclosure of Urdhr.

Reflected upon earth, this meeting place of peace became the sacrosanct *Thing* in honour of the justice witnessed in that boundary and acted upon by the gods themselves. It is not without some sense of irony that this very place the *Nornenburg* became the site chosen for the most controversial trials in the wake of humankind's warring upon itself in the latter half of the last century.

The chthonic element in Norse Mythology finds expression through the form of the serpentine dragon or *Wyrm*, gnawing constantly at the root that lies in *Niflheimhr,* though its purpose remains undetermined. Modern Western culture has become readily influenced by its erroneous perception of the mechanics of time envisioned as being upheld in classical periods. Noted all too frequently as *past* (that which has gone before), *present* (that which is) and future (that which will be), they easily became attached to cognate impressions regarding associations with the three Norns, placing them as *Urdhr [past], Verdhandi [present], and Skulde [future?].*

This perception, overly stated and frequently, fails to grasp the simplicity of the mind set of a people for whom only the moment is significant, wherein all things led to and onwards from it. It is therefore incorrect. Common Fate was the mechanics of application for the collective termed Orlog and Wyrd was reserved for the fate of the individual. Orlog = Cosmic Me: Ond = Cosmic Breath: Od= inspiration. Teutonic time-sense however, was conceptualized as a *becoming.* This refined a focus to only *that-which-is* as encompassing all that has transpired before, albeit as a network of finely woven cloth as the warp and weft together with *that-which-is-becoming,* the ever changing instant, the singular moment of the greater Orlog. The combination of these two generates the third, in which the rightness of those actions is simultaneously assessed, judged and re-dressed accordingly. This was the Dark Age mindset of the Teutonic culture. No future tense existed in this 'age of a man.'[lxviii]

The Norns/Nornir

Within the whole Northern Tradition three fundamental principles exist, much revered and without which we would have little understanding of the philosophies concerning destiny.[lxix]They effectively equate to the [Aryan] Three Mothers, holding elements of Air, Water and Earth. These are distinct from the three Hebraic Mothers of Air Water and Fire, adding further confirmation to this perception as that held by Roy Bowers and John [Jones] of the Three Mothers holding all [spiritual] elements except Fire, alone belonging to the elder God: of Luciferic forms.

The Nornir as weavers are frequently associated with the Fates, the Moirae (of ancient Greece) and Roman Parcae. Three women sit and spin the threads of fate weaving their tapestry of becoming, severing the threads of life at there *allotted* moment. In similar guise I suggest the Valkyrie as weavers; Skulde, the youngest and fairest Valkyrie is also of the Nornir. Spinning, as a magical skill, was an attested gift of the Nornir, shared among The Fates and Frigga from whom they acquire their silken skeins that weave all destinies including those of the gods. Within the great cosmos of being, all are subject to the laws of the Nornir. By some strange paradox, it is recorded how the Nornir live vicariously through human interchange and find their best expression through the patterns they weave among them. Hence, if favoured, you are woven a long and interesting life. As guardian spirits assigned at birth to all new souls, it is their jurisdiction that decides whether it be bound to weal or woe.

Atropas is beautiful beyond vision, yet is veiled [apportions lots]; *Clotho* is ancient [spinner of thread from Her Distaff to spindle] and the final Nornir, *Lachesis* is fixed, immovable, an anchor to the others [measurer of life with her rod-spear]. All three are said to preserve the pivotal Harmony of the Universe bound in gossamer threads. However, a role they share with the gods, bids them all to the Well of Wyrd where the Nornir reside among them, to debate the fates of humankind. [lxx] Through their artful craft, cherished opinion, law and belief, manifest forces spin tightly over the affairs of mortal man. Through those works do we learn of their guardianship of the bright *Well of Wyrd*, the fount of time and wisdom and of their execution in the laws in all realms of consciousness?

Here form the waters of all things past into the 'All Present.'

This holy Well of Wyrd is also known as *Urðarbrunnr, Urdhr's Well,* or the well of that which was. (hind-sight)

The second Well of Wyrd found at the root of the great world tree Yggdrasil is *Hvergelmir* (bubbling/ boiling spring) the primal well from which the first waters flowed.

The Third and final Well is *Mimmisbrunnr* (Mimir's Well) the place where knowledge and foresight may be obtained.

All three wells express the northern cosmology through the manifest potencies of time and being.

"The Nornir dwell by the Well of Wyrd and are said to have a shining hall there, they are often depicted as three cloaked figures, almost indistinguishable from each other. Each day the Gods cross over the rainbow bridge and gather at the Well to debate and cast judgements, testifying to the Well's importance as a place of truth and source of law. Any beings who bathe within the Well of Wyrd are said to emerge shining white, like the membrane of an egg; and a pair of swans (said to be the ancestors of all other swans), are said to feed at the well each day. Interestingly, some accounts state that Munnin, one of Odhin's ravens, is

pure white – Munnin is the raven of memory and, perhaps, he too drinks at the Well."[lxxi]

Within the great root of Yggdrasil in the Realm of Asgardhr, the Nornir behold a shadowy existence by the Well of Wyrd, *Urdhr's* well, revealing the cosmic wellspring of life, destiny, and justice known as *'Urdarbrunnr.'* Tending its waters preserved and healed the very sap and virtue of this cosmic tree, compromised by the very act of decay and rot of manifest life itself. A daily anointing with white clay from the spring together with the pure, gleaming water drawn from the well, misted the earth in turn, with dew so potent, the milk yielded by deer grazing upon the moisture laden branches was honey'd mead – the poets inspiration, divine manna and elixir of life. So smoothly the poultice is laid upon the decaying bark of Yggdrassil to extend its life and fecundity. These primal forms are better known as the jutuns, the titans/ogress.

Urdhr = yr rune

Urdhr, oldest of the three, whose name translates to: *that which was*-origin.

Urdhr (and all other variants including) *Wurd* (Old High German), *Wryd* (Anglo-Saxon), *Weird* (English), *Urth, Urtha, Urdhr, Urda, Ertha* are frequently used where any general inference to fate is stated, yet She forms only one facet of this triplicity. In fact the English word earth stems from that root form. She suggests *initial patterning* of the life matrix.

Verðandi/Weorthunde =gyfu rune

Verðandi is said to select the threads woven by Urdhr from the fibres of the earth and tree bark, weaving them together into the great tapestry of becoming, of all being. Each person has their own destiny to fulfill; each small narrative woven into the greater whole via a myriad choices and possibilities. Un-distracted by events unfurling before her, She embodies the principle of mindfulness. Verðandi/Weorthunde as the second facet of three, signifies the actual point and moment of *'Being.'*

Skulde = laguz rune

Skulde, youngest of the Nornir and true Valkyrie is a warrior maiden whose name translates as debt–necessity and *that which must be* all of which implies destiny in the fullest sense of its meaning. Skulde cuts the threads that bind the soul to its earthly form, releasing it to bear its karma in life. Skulde is also the overseer of knots or oaths, the very nodes of intersection of shared or crossed destiny.

To renege an oath is to invoke the very depths of chaos upon oneself under the law that prevails against. Such an act undermines the evolution of a soul in harmony with Wryd. Skulde [skogul] bears a shield and wears a shining helmet and cloak of swan feathers. Valkyrie are said to shift in groups of three.

Skulde oversees the first and last necessity: that of repaying the final *debt* of death which all living things owe from their first breath. For this reason, She is the most revered and held in the highest awe, the one credited with the measure of all. She rightly holds the Doom as her gift. Her deeds are foretold over and over through her handmaidens aptly known as Skalds. Their poetry was uttered in shamanic trances, portraying a visionary future, borne importantly from the events of the past.

They refer often to the Soma, the inspiring mead, the elixir of the gods, no less, the Poison Chalice. Skulde is Valkyrie most often associated with divine Soma, being named in a poem that describes the component parts of Soma. Intriguingly, this is given as 3/1 parts *Mead to Whiskey.* This invites an assumption that all three Nornir are the divine elixir present within the mead, possibly even as air, water and earth, completing in whiskey as *uisage beatha,* the fiery draught as the literal *waters of life.*

Clearly, this kiss of death taken from the lips of one so divine impels the soul to follow.

Voluspa: 13th century Poetic Edda:

Sá hon valkyrjur	She saw Valkyries
vítt um komnar,	come from far and wide,
görvar at ríða	ready to ride
til Goðþjóðar.	to Goðþjóð.
Skuldhelt skildi,	Skuldeheld a shield,
en Skögul önnur,	and Skögul was another,
Gunnr, Hildr, Göndul	Gunnr, Hildr, Göndul
ok Geirskögul.	and Geirskögul.

Perennial Philosophy Regarding Truth

"The notion of a universal principle of natural order has been compared to similar ideas in other cultures, such as Asha in Avestan religion, Rta in Vedic Religion, and Maat in Ancient Egyptian Religions. The word is the proper name of the divinity Asha, the personification of Truth and Righteousness.

Ana corresponds to an objective, material reality which embraces all of existence. This cosmic force is imbued also with morality, as verbal Truth, and Righteousness, action conforming to the moral order.

In the [Gnostic] literature of the Mandeans, an angelic being, has the responsibility of weighing the souls of the deceased to determine their worthiness, using a set of scales."[lxxii]

Looking now to the Tree of Life, its central pillar of Grace again unites all the virtues of Maat, upheld through Orlog as the sacred Mé [Oaths/justice, balance, law and order] anchored to and defined by the Nowl Star in the Heavens through the *Gardhr Tree* itself defined by the Stang raised upon the Earth below. The Tau itself is a symbol expressing victory in combat, but also death, especially as burials and cremations. Thor's hammer is a stylised vajra, an Irminsul as transmitter of Virtue. It resembles the middle pillar, Otz Chim.

Irminsul – Pillar of Grace.

As above so below – Just as She binds the forces of Chaos from the Void presumed by our ancestors to exist beyond the boundaries of our spiral galaxy, with Cosmic Law and Order, the Stang in the North is that upon which Fenris is bound. Chaos rules this sector of the Compass. The Mound is the domain of the forces of death, destruction and chaos, but also of life renewed, since through silken bindings, Tyr, now rooted as the Nowl Star, re-defines Fenris as the ouroboros, the Midgardhr World Serpent that which stalks beyond the boundary of Order. In keeping with the myth of Ragnarok and the destruction of our Sun by Fenris, it is extremely interesting to consider that an optical double star appears within the constellation of Lupus.

There is also a blue giant – Beta Lupi, 13,600 times brighter than our Sun though its distance gives it the appearance of being substantially dimmer. Nearing the end of its life it is destined to become a red supergiant and then, ultimately, a supernova! [lxxiii]

The Binding of Fenris by Tyr

In vain hope Odhin led the mighty Fenris into the Halls of Asgardhr; to pacify him was his sole desire, to tame this Mighty Beast of Chaos. One by one, the gods all shrank away none daring to approach, save one, whose heart was Compassion. Thus Tyr alone fed the beast. But to no avail, for the beast would not be soothed or pacified and grew daily in ferocity and size. Foresworn were they to harm not another such as they, and so a resolve through wisdom was sought. To bind him fast then, but who would be equal to such a task? Each attempt further enraged the beast as chains and bindings of the finest forgings and castings were shattered.

"Twice did the Æsir strive to bind?
Twice did they fetters powerless find;
Iron or brass of no avail,
Naught, save through magic, could prevail."

[Valhalla -J. C. Jones].

Naught but an enchanted thread, woven from the finest spindle of the dark elves, of thoughts and wishes fair, of dreams and breath en-twinned within the silken gossamer of the fairest girdle, adornment of Tyr.

"Gleipnir, at last,
By Dark Elves cast,
In Svart-alf-heim, with strong spells wrought,
To Odhin was by Skirnir brought:
As soft as silk, as light as air,
Yet still of magic power most rare."

[Valhalla -J. C. Jones].

With Gleipnir then the gods challenged Fenris a final time; but Fenris, perplexed by this delicate rope suspected another stronger chain concealed. Adamant that none should approach unless a show of hands be given, of good intent to reveal, no blade or shaft of mal intent concealed. To pledge his faith, this open hand be brought close enough to jaw to bite. Tyr stepped forth, unafraid, and without fear laid hand upon his fanged jaw; such soothing tender tones she uttered as galdr magics strengthened the silken girdle, as it slid betwixt them both. Onto and around Fenris it was spun, and fastened tightly. Gleipnir secure, the gods rejoiced, but Tyr was caught in her own web, as her hand became forever locked within the jaws of chaos. Rooted thus, her movements thereon in were bound to the beast, a pillared post twixt heaven and earth. Together, as one, they would dance for all time in the heavens above, spinning without motion, stars to illuminate the void beyond even the Halls of Asgardhr.

Glorious Anima Mundi, Vain Fenris - arcane expressions of the forces of Law and Order, of Chaos and the taming of Chaos. Only the beautiful Maiden may tame the Beast; Durga and Babylon ride the Beast of Chaos; Maat holds all within the palm of Her hand; The Maiden too as with hand extended in tenderness bridles the Unicorn, the wild element of destruction close to her body within her sacred bower, the enclosure of the Maiden. The starry realms above reflect the sacred boundary below. Rapunzal has spun her silken tresses, she has loosened them, they fall unbound upon the prince, her lover and nemesis. She draws him to her, locked within her keep. The beautiful Maid and the rapacious Beast. Her stoic wisdom (law & order) he sought; his strength and freedom (chaos) she sought. Thus balanced, they remain, the Ivory tower, the sacred gardhr, the hidden enclosure of the self, the Horn Childe.

Chapter Twelve

TYR: HIGH GOD

An inscription on a 3rd century altar from a Roman fort at Housesteads, Hadrian's Wall bears the name of *'Mars Thingsus'* (*Thincsus*). Possibly erected by Frisian mercenaries stationed there, it suggests a common synthesis where soldiers living and fighting in such close active proximity to the practices of other, readily adapted the many idiosyncratic vagaries and subtleties of those tribes and clans they encountered.

For these '*People*' the manifest Virtue that in our time would define *god* could best be described as a potency inherently resident within what were essentially tutelary beings, frequently accompanied by a host of otherworld spirits. The absolute overarching consummate *divine essence* that has become translated detrimentally as the 'God' would have been utterly alien to them with regard to the monotheistic oligarchy of the post-Christian era. Tacitus summates the import of a priesthood associated with the *Thing* to whom Clan elders would defer in all matters involving judgment, being deemed in accord to the *Will* as expressed through battle and combat. [lxxiv]

Old English Rune Poems signify *Tiw/Tir* to mean *glory.* This rune was popularly inscribed on Anglo-Saxon cremation urns in preference to other symbols available. Closer inspection highlights a perception of profound subtlety regarding their sense of the divine that only later become transmuted into a god when awarded a literal personification previously absent from the cognitive appreciation of the nebulous, somatic 'All.'

According to a 12th century account, a Patron Goddess *Cisaria* was founded by Swabian tribes as a defence against Roman incursions.[lxxv] In keeping with classical myth, it has been erroneously assumed that Cisaria/*Zisa* typified the stereotypical role of consort rather than a primary and female deity. Tacitus made note of a Germanic tribe of *Isis* worshippers for whom there no doubt this confirms more about his familiarity with a female deity of that prominence than it does to one that in all probability relates to Zisa. Jacob Grimm similarly formed this conclusion, asserting an etymological link connecting Zisa to Ziu directly, and by default Zeus.

Tacitus repeated his prejudicial oversight in further presumptions regarding other deities, namely *Tyr*, setting an historically inaccurate precedent for others to follow. Certainly, late Icelandic literature completely ignored earlier lateral cognates found in *Tuisto/Tir/Tiewas* to portray Tyr[lxxvi] as a son of Odhin in the (in the Prose Edda) and of Hymir (from the Poetic Edda). Previously, Tyr had been long perceived as a celestial and ultimate divine luminary, overseer of justice and truth.

Odhin: Alfaðir, Alföðr – All-Father but more interestingly as Aldaföðr - Father of Men.[lxxvii]

The Old Norse name *Tyr* was actually a generic noun meaning *god* and may be noted in the suffix to many of the epithets assigned to Odhin. For example - *Hangatyr*, the *god* of the hanged. Used in this way, the essence in the form of an emanation imbues another form. In the Eddic poem *Lokasenna* though it does not refer to Týr directly, Zisa is again mentioned.[lxxviii] Further examples define Hrafn*týr* as raven- god and Val*týr* - god of the slain; again these are later attributes assigned to Odhin and do not relate to gender, only the various qualities or virtues awarded by this divine being.

Dyēus (also Dyēus phater) is the reconstructed chief deity of the (PIE pantheon) *sky*, a position mirrored in the position of the patriarch or monarch in that society. Later gods share etymological links with Dyēus.[lxxix] Revealingly for this study is the *related but distinct* (IE) word for deity: *deiwos* Latinized as *deus.*[lxxx]

This Latin form finds continuity of usage within the English variants - *divine*, *deity*, and *day* hence we find the original preserved within the day of *Tīwaz*. It is also linked to Old Norse *tívar* (gods), exampled in *Tiveden*-Wood [gardhr edin of the God/Tyr?]. Pantheons of individual mythologies (drawing from original roots - PIE) evolved slowly and attributes of *Dyēus* became re-assigned to the ever-changing mutable god-forms appropriate for the era. In classical mythology though, Dyēus remained stubbornly the pinnacle of hierarchy in contrast to the decayed form Dyēus became in Vedic mythology, becoming a very abstract god-form.

Intrinsic qualities of certain deities, if popular were acquired and given prominence in another, becoming transferred to other gods such as Agni[lxxxi] and Indra.[lxxxii] Again we discover very interesting associations and links between *Deus* - divine/light/shining and *Dyēus* to the original meaning of divine/day, combining as divine daylight. With regard to our own mythos and understanding of the underlying premise of Lucifer Mythologically and theologically who is the divine light of day, the solar day star [akin to others across Anatolia and Asia].

Obviously this is a powerful and controversial assertion, but one that restores *Tyr* as an original, transcendental position, without form of gender or the humanlike qualities attributed to the pantheon of gods and goddesses developed during the Middle Ages. Whether these were influenced by negative feedback from the Sagas or developed the complex families independently is impossible to secure now so many hundreds of years have obfuscated these events.

A rare, shining gem may be gleaned from this fruitful search, increasing the possibility of Tyr as a superior force of jurisdiction, above even the gods, meting out justice and judgment in the form of karma – the fate we engage through action.

Numerous bracteates[lxxxiii] feature stylized portraits of Germanic Kings with mythological characteristics much influenced by Roman coinage motifs. Their use is unknown, but there are strong divinatory elements present and protective iconic imagery.

Accompanied with horse, spear and birds a figure identified with aspects of Wodan/Wotan appeared later, somewhat transformed as Odhin in 13th century depictions within the Poetic Edda. These bracteates are therefore invaluable resources for determining the runic inscriptions, the iconic imagery and their implicit Germanic paganisms.[1]

Delving further into the realms of Tyr, a discovery is found, a treasure in the form of a melody,[lxxxiv] from the 7th century, believed to be a war-cry in fact; though this is unproven, named *Tyribus* (Tyr have us). The Barditus, mentioned by Tacitus is a particularly chilling war-cry executed over the shield (or bort) when raised to chin level. This serves two purposes, it increases the volume, but more importantly emphasizes the invocation rendered to the Shield maiden, the warrior protectress and Clan tutelary spirit to be with them and to bear them home, dead or alive.

Attempts to connect the phrase *teribus an teriodin* to an Old English cry - *Týr hæbbe us, e Týr e Oðinn* translated as *May [the god] Tyr keep us, both Tyr and Odin* is another example of how names and their usage have become confused. Since the cry would have included the English forms of Tiw and Wodan, rather than those deific forms of the pantheons familiar to the Scandinavian and Norse, Thor and Odhin are unlikely candidates in this matter. However, Charles Mackey's description of the ballad defers to their *defensive use specifically against invaders.*

Though unpopular as an interpretation among peers, this is expected when paradigms are challenged seriously. Perhaps it is time to re-claim and restore such understandings that remain so important to our appreciation of this vital potency. A revealing list within Appendix One compares the qualities beside Odhin's that suggest a startling paradigm where it is in fact Odhin as the usurper, a title befitting a deity of invading/colonizing peoples who inevitably imposed their own warrior/gender ethic. Odhin is certainly a later presence in the sagas.

Looking at the rune shape itself as a glyph, it is almost a facsimile of a pillar, poetically supporting the vault of heaven, a great pillar named as *Irminsul.* The Tree/wood of Irmin/Tyr - the Anglo-Saxon equivalent to the Asherah pole. The great gardhr tree is indeed the manifest and cosmological guise of the Ultimate Creatrix whose glorious essence – Tyr as Cosmic order, exemplifies. Reaching up into the heavens, the North Star is transfixed. The Nowl Star! of Tyr. It indicates perhaps the Tau cross and its inherent connotations therein. As Tiewas, the sword deity of battle triumphant, victory is evoked.

As the nail of might, light and virtue, it magically complements the chthonic Ingwaz, whence it draws the promethean light at midsummer to conquer the darkness in the Arctic Circle, the very Land of the Midnight Sun! Of course, within Norse belief, Wolves represent chaos, death and destruction. Rune poems refer to this when speaking of Tyr as the defender of order against chaos. Bound intrinsically thereafter, inseparable from each other as eternal cosmic foes, Tyr is thereafter referred to as the *Leavings of the Wolf (the beast).* In fact this metaphor is simply a poetic kenning for *glory.* This of course ties in seamlessly to the-afore mentioned reference to Tyr as *glory.* This is further emphasized in an Anglo-Saxon rune poem in which the rune *Tir,* as *glory* refers to and describes a constellation or star essential to mariners for navigation:

"Tiris a certain sign; it keeps faith well with noblemen over the mists of night; it never fails."

Perhaps in considering the erroneous associations that cumulatively demonstrate a composite figure totally unrelated and unrecognizable to those persons to whom this deity would have been venerated in the form known to them, we should here emphasize again that *Tiw* and its cognates simply mean god, or the god. The fact that to the Romans this term for them became applied to a male deity should not perpetuate the deceptive presumption that others shared a similar and restricted perception of their god. Sharing veneration for the god applied to the head of the Roman pantheon which for them happens to be male yet for whom is viewed as being without distinct gender by the Anglo-Saxons, is a very different paradigm to sharing veneration for the god whose descriptive term actually assigns a distinctly *male* gender to that god. Deus is neutral.

Tacitus is merely one of many to have done so, when he made comparison with *Tir* as a deity with martial potencies to the Roman god of war, Mars. Countless others compounded this error since in literature that has swamped and glossed over the beautiful and poetic inscription to *Tir* that makes no actual mention to gender; in fact where the merest inference is made, it is to an androgynous being of neither particular sex at all. Roman ethics would never have granted such importance to a female, the closest of whom in their own ranks was Minerva and the Greek Athena, whose intriguing martial qualities manifest through her patronage; as tutelary goddess of Athens, she is a protectress, a defender no less. She presents an effective cognate to Britannia, who has bona-fide links back to *Ida* within Anglo-Saxons settled in Britain.[lxxxv]

Making the shift back towards Anatolia and the origins of the arcane myth of the homeland, of grandmother *Ida*, we find there another clue in the form of the Hittite and Hattic god of the sun and sky who bears many similarities to the Luwian language[lxxxvi] forms also known as *Tiwaz* (non-genitive.[lxxxvii]) or *Tijaz*. Exceptions are present where this god of judgment is depicted bearing a crooked staff and a glorious crown, designed to represent a winged sun. All traits are contra to those of Odhin, who adopts only some of them, as required by those People whose *need* required this transmutation:

unipolar/fixed/associated with 'thing'/binder of oaths/ hand of justice/law/order/mind/separator of heaven and earth/tamer of beast/battlefoe/sword & spear/victory/silence/linked to iron, thorn, Aries

& ram/animate force/will and desire [for life] / the religious instinct within humankind/transcendental quality/ keeper of the threefold mystery = Virtue

In northern countries, a folk name for aconite, one among the trio of banes attributed to Hekate and to the Fates, is *Tyr's Helm*; Given that another of its folk names is also *Wolfsbane*, I find this connection very intriguing. Yet another name associated with this particular bane is *Auld wives Cap*. Atropa belladonna is clearly the province of the beautiful but deadly Skulde/Skogul, leaving a choice of hemlock or mandrake for Geiramul/Verdandi.

The Saxon form of the World Tree is infinitely more profound than the Norse Yggdrassil. Irmin is accepted by numerous scholars in addition to Jacob Grimm as being an avatar or epithet for Tyr. This is further strengthened by the connections even with Norse language and myth via *Immin*: Iomungrund – the World Serpent, the ground of being, and earth shaker! There is, however, NO fixed expression or interpretation of Tyr as anything beyond a rather vague force and form, shining resplendence, a nebulous force of will and desire to be, to exist – at its simplest it means a [genderless] GOD! This may be read as *Virtue.* [Ios is a Frisian rune for chaos/world serpent] This iconic pillar then, is clearly the original serpent stang! The holy gardhr tree of wisdom, the whispering wind of inspiration and vital odic force. It is flux and stasis as She, the mistress of Fate decrees. Eveoh He, *Eve* is She, Mother of all life and wisdom. The eye and the hand of Qayin in the truest sense. Q, the occult glyph for queen, the utterer, and ayin is the all-seeing eye. The single eye of the Norns and the hand of Fate!

Tyr, Tiu, or Ziu according to different mythologists, placed in a triad with Odhin and Frigga, the 'queen' and Mother of all gods. Sometimes it is a beautiful giantess whose name is unknown, that becomes Mother, yet it is She who is the personification of the raging sea, The tempest known as Guilvig! Tyr represents *martial honour*, as distinct from martial conduct, a distinction of considerable importance in assisting us to better understand the subtle nuances of this much overlooked personage. Tyr although one of the twelve principal deities of Asgardhr, appears to have had no special dwelling yet in the halls of Valhalla one of the 12 thrones in the great council hall of Gladsheimhr was reserved for Her.

"The hall Gladsheimhr, which is built of gold;
Where are in circle ranged twelve golden chairs,
And in the midst one higher, Odin's throne."

BALDER DEAD (Matthew Amold)

Tyr as the valorisation of courage was frequently invoked by the various nations of the North, to ensure victory in actual combat. Tiu - Tuesday. Under the name of Ziu, celebratory dances still use the thin rapper swords to create the central rose, the binding thorn and bloom of one's word/oath. Tyr was venerated as the principal divinity of the Swabians, the sword was considered a distinctive attribute, and in high honour they held great sword dances, still extant in parts of Yorkshire. Upon completion of the dance, all swords become combined into the shape of a rose or wheel [the spinning wheel, Flaming Crown shield and flower of honour]. The sword point was further considered so sacred that it became customary to register oaths upon it. Once more, the arcane principle of Nemesis sings out in this image.

"Come hither, gentlemen,
And lay your hands again upon my sword;
Never to speak of this that you have heard,
Swear by my sword."

HAMLET (Shakespeare)

An alleged feature of the worship of Tyr among the Franks and some other Northern nations recounts the sacrificial acts undertaken by its priesthood, named somewhat improbably as the Druids or *Godi/Godhi.* Yet even this term has its roots in the earliest Sanskrit form of the word Goda (see appendices) as the administrator and guardian of all due and relevant sacrifice within the devotional context of an ancient and sacred arte.

"Sig-runes thou must know,
If victory (sigr) thou wilt have,
And on thy sword's hilt rist them;
Some on the chapes,
Some on the guard,
And twice name the name of Tyr."

LAY OF SIGDRIFA (Thorpe's tr.)

Other bright and solar divinities have been compared to Tyr, namely Saxnot and Cheru; but these are again localized forms, personal names that refer to the greater ambivalence, the whole. Yet the links to protection through arms is again asserted.

"This very sword a ray of light
Snatched from the Sun!"

VALHALLA (J. C. Jones)

Tyr's Sword

According to an ancient legend, *Cheru*' owned a sword, fashioned by the dwarvish sons of Ivaldi, who had also made Odin's sacred spear Gungnir. Into the care of his people this mighty weapon was entrusted, announcing that whosoever possessed would be victorious in battle. Due to a startling prophecy surrounding the sword, it was guarded with extreme caution. Nonetheless, it vanished, mysteriously.

A Seeress, familiar with the enormity of the consequence for the world and for the present wielder of the enchanted sword of *Cheru* 'had refused to announce its whereabouts. Another legend recounts how after the conversion of the Heathens from their paganism, this sword and all its qualities for weal or woe, became transferred over to the Archangel St. Michael, who has wielded it ever since.

Tyr, synonymous with bravery and wisdom, was never mentioned without comment upon the milk-white maidens, the Valkyries, gathers of the fallen beside Her.

"The god Tyr sent
Göndul and Skogul
To choose a king
Of the race of Ingve,
To dwell with Odin
In roomy Valhal."

NORSE MYTHOLOGY (R. B. Anderson)

This is the Clan version of the now famous Mask Prayer. It is clearly not a leaf mask built upon the face, but a facsimile of origin. A map of ages. It re-minds/re-binds *memory* to *thought*. It instills within the psyche, the place of origin and being through the cosmological expression within its few simple but poignant lines.

Tyr may easily be invoked in line with all such qualities commonly assigned to Maat. For She is undeniably cast in the mold of Maat.

The Leaf Mask Blessing

O Thou who created the earth and the heavens
Who separated Order from Chaos
And Time from Eternity,
We call to thee
Thou who listens to our deepest voice,
Thou who inspires our ancestral wisdom
Thou who shines forth the pleasing light
And who protects us from the baneful might of the destroyer
We call to thee
Pray let us speak always with
Thy inner voice of spiritual things,
And may love be our guiding light
In the name of Lucifer,
And of the Dark Mothers,
Whose spirit moves all.
Thoet Se!

It is vital to remember that fables and legends are the repositories of wisdom and lore, not the source of them. They are multi-faceted, having many layers of meaning that are often mutually compatible, but not always. As tales, they are not always as they seem, nor as true as given, nor the bias as obvious; so much of the material gifted in the Norse Sagas and Eddas is heavily overlaid with Christian glosses.

Scholars are vigilant in their attempts to amend these early errors and are re-defining all subtleties previously obfuscated by bad translations and judicial editing. Odhin appears later than Tyr from whom he retrieves the source knowledge of the runes and the teachings as the primal Mother to become 'All Father.' Irminsul is the very pillar of wisdom, the serpent stang drawn from the tree (yard arm?) upon which he 'hung' himself to gather up this worldly wisdom.

The thread that we have painstakingly followed indicates this as far from being wildly speculative, but a very real possibility. So little scholarly research is available on Tyr concerning the origins of this enigmatic deity, so it remains nebulous and exposed to a great deal of corruption that has systematically undermined its true character and worth within the Northern tradition and our Clan's Mythos.

Attempts to relate Tyr to Jupiter/Zeus through this root: Devas/Deivos /Djevs/Dyeus/Deus/Theos [bright mind] rather than Tiwas/Ziu/Ciza/Zeus, reveal poor scholarship and an over-eagerness to actually ignore the etymology in favour of popularist perception, oft repeated to the detriment of truth. No more no less. The Shining One eventually became sexed as 'he' where that early root developed through increasing adaptation within the Roman and Greek pantheons despite *deus/ deva* having no gender, originally. ONE divine being became two sexed beings, albeit briefly, then as culture required, became determined as a patriarchal head, best exemplified by the warring factions during the transition from European Bronze ages into Iron Ages. In the East too, such paradigm shifts were implemented as Zoroaster joined the tide of new philosophers re-working old terms to present them more appropriately contra to those around them who continued with the outmoded forms as they perceived them. Devas were demoted to devils and the opposing asuras [demons] were elevated to angelic status as beings of Truth and of Illumination. It's all about how things are understood and applied to the culture aligned within a pertinent Cosmology.

When philosophies are taken from one culture and adapted from those of another they typically become subject to many reversals of identity and purpose. Venus, almost universally accepted as female, remains very much a masculine figure to Arabic peoples. Because of these shifts, some academics have stressed the transience of concepts and the foolhardy acceptance of superficial yet deep-rooted bias; nonetheless, their views have been sidelined so as not to counter the Judaic/Christian legerdemain over time. The Most High god of the anunnaki, Anu, provides another example of a 'male' sky father perceived very differently in Ireland as the archaic Mother.

In consideration of the now much obfuscated gender of the primal and titanic Tyr, it has proved extremely helpful to list all those qualities ascribed to Tyr alongside the main female deities of major cultures in the distant past. When compared to the qualities given to contemporary male deities, it can be shown how consistently those that quantify the divine feminine are in the remit of Tyr, and no male deity.

This matter of cultural diffusion, of influences brought to bear upon religious beliefs over time and space as people evolve, provides a clearer perspective of ancestry, beliefs and foundations, now revealed through a better understanding of those cosmologies, especially with regard to their relevance, here and now. Our Northern ancestry is peeled back as it were. So let us not forget the Eddas and Sagas were rewritten by monks and it was certainly NOT in their interest to have the Supreme Being presented as either unisexual being or a female. Even the translations of the Icelandic writer Snorri Sturluson are now being scrutinized by academics for his excessive and sometimes brutal liberties at variance with comparative and original sources.

Particular passages overwritten by monks present Tyr very much in the mar*tyr*ed[lxxxviii] light of *male* sacrifice; a stance they similarly adopted in their articulation of Odhin's trial (not literal death) upon the tree. But that myth is slowly disintegrating. Although neither of them is a Christ figure in any sense, the monks tried so very hard to make them appear so, to the extent where certain anomalies were totally ignored and dismissed. The thread, and all matters relating to law and justice, the girdle and the necklace are definitive examples of female Virtue since time immemorial; as such they are undisputedly feminine tools. This is precisely why Roy Bowers refers to the *Ring* as the necklace, bearing links even to the bright stones of Freya's *Brisingamen*. Freya however, though a major goddess, is not THE Creatrix; having no primality, she is subsumed into Aesir domination, assimilated as a cultural and somewhat localized aspect of a synthesis of ancestral, tutelary aspect within the Sublime Triplicity of Fate.

Similarly, another misleading enterprise involving days of the week, lists Tuesday as having associations with Tyr. Yet this occurred quite late and meant nothing other than the name of a *god* being assigned to a day of the week. Tyr's qualities have always vacillated between Mars and Jupiter because, conventionally speaking, it is uncertain where to place this enigmatic being. Clearly, She belongs 'in-between' them, literally and figuratively. For the Clan, having its Mythos expressed through the Compass, this is quite a significant association bridging three aspects together along a specific axis. Tiphareth [centre point] - Sun; Geburah [NW] - Mars and Chesed [SE] – Jupiter. Curiously, when stood with our backs in the North, this sphere of influence Tyr exerts is left, as Ida, the left channel of the body.

When laying the Compass, a cord is attached to the central staff, to form a groove, a furrow by a blade tied to the outer edge of the cord –all to delineate the sacred 'Thing,' the assembly of peace and arbitration under the auspices of Tyr subject to Her judgments and justice. When placed centrally, the stang points both right and left of Tyr in the planetary qualities of Mars and Jupiter, and also in Geburah as severity and Chesed as Mercy, forming a horizontal slightly curved cross bar [and ingress and egress to the mound of Chaos] to the unseen vertical bar stretching from hearth to altar/stang in the north. This Northern Tau is Tyr, Justice and

Compassion – Grace -the triune triplicity of all levels of the gardhr tree upon the Stang. The Masked Stang merely places the eternal as manifest within the boundary of the present.

Many years ago now, we had watched as John explained this arcane dance beneath the gardhr tree where decades hence, Roy had invoked the winds, chanting the rune sounds carried high aloft the sparking flames within a central hearth. And though not fully understood, or appreciated at that moment, John instilled the seeds that have finally borne the fruit of dawning as we may now comprehend fully the purpose of a boundary that is not a boundary, a mound that harnesses chaos and the sacral ground around the hearth, where no brother or sister may draw arms against another, and why peace reigns supreme there. He said we would come to fully understand who the three are that reside in unison in the Northern regions, why Lucifer is Chaos, the ever prowling Wolf seeking to devour His own Bright self in the moment of his becoming, and why we must hold that moment in stasis [Isa] until all humankind also understands the beauty of this Truth, revealed through their own filters and cultural principles.

That Tyr was originally twinned for a short time with Zisa, a Shakti who later vanished from all record, adds further interest in her identification. The Gardhr is also a rune denoting "spear" and contains all the other runes in the Anglo-Saxon rune set. It signifies the boundary and the centre point. Curiously, this great stave reaching upwards into the heavens around which the stars rotate in balance and harmony by Tyr's act asserts the pole as the Gardh tree; Irminsul is Tyr, the pillar that links heaven to earth. Anchored by the Nowl/North star, She is bound through Her own Wyrd to the eternal cycle, the revolution of the 12 zodiacal constellations of the celestial canopy, the Halls of Asgardhr. All orbit in unison and harmony – chaos lies beyond the perimeter of stability. This is the most basic and accepted of all perennial cosmologies. There is much lore in this heresy.

Of course his numerous epithets form a composite of the many attributes he assumes over time from other deities that precede him. Tyr is the name invoked for victory, for justice. As the Nowl Star, Tyr is considered to reside in the *Land of the Midnight Sun, Thule*, the favoured mythical landscape, wherein light conquers darkness through perpetual dawn. Metaphorically, it is the light of illumination, of realization.

Tyr then is a 'god' of primal titanic antiquity, but really an arcane and profound active /manifest principle of TRUTH of karma in fact. This

Multifaceted Supreme She, the All becomes manifest through Her Laws, administered through the Fates, otherwise known as the *Me* and Karma.

They rule the destinies of all, even the gods. In thinking of Hekate, the triune force named by Roy Bowers as a *close approximation* to the more personal and intimate names we know Her by, it is extremely enlightening to note how even the feast days for *Tyr* and *Hekate* are shared. Both are honoured on the 2nd February and August 13th.

Chapter Thirteen

CONCLUSION: THE ORDER OF BEING

Again Hesiod's Theogony records how the Fates were once considered as the daughters of Zeus and Themis, the sisters of the Horae yet also the offspring of Nyx, the goddess of Night. He names them: *Clotho, Lachesis, and Atropos.*

- Clotho the Spinner, is closest to *Geiramul/Weorthunde/Gyfu*
- Lachesis is *Tyr/Wyrd/Yr*
- Atropos as She who severs the cord, represents the inevitable end to life in *Skogul/Skulde/Lagu*

Clotho selects the thread that Lachesis measures for Atropos to cut. "*That binds the Staff that's owned by the Maid*" springs to mind here, from the poem attributed to Roy Bowers named 'the House that Jack built;' Jack being the devil of course. The Robin, son of arte.

The inevitable Fate of all humanity, the gods and even the Cosmos itself, is known as *Orlog* (Old Norse for cycle of fate, derived from *Lagu*-origin/void); this pre-destined destruction is the fabled event *Ragnarok.* This is forecast to take place again upon the plains of Ida - as in life-so in death. This level of fate is clearly overarching, distinct yet inclusive of the *Wyrd* said to affect each individual. Orlog is best described as the equilibrating point between Chaos and Order, the Law that harmonizes *all* opposing forces acting throughout the flux of our Universe. This primality has been awarded many names and forms across time and geography. Suffice to say, we may safely equate it as the Law, the Word, the *Mè* - The

Tablets of Destiny no less, shaped and honed by the Ultimate Primality of She, who is without name and form.

Yr; lagu; gyfu; are the three runes of destiny assigned to the Stang, representing these triple forces sourced in the primality of a past beyond memory, from the first beings and ancestors to the *people* linked through memory; from the gods to those *priests* who hearken to the wisdoms of the *Word* and from the demi-gods and heroes of old who inspire our valour and integrity to protect and shield the virtue of these arcane truths in sacred reverence, away from things deemed profane. These then, are the Fates, the Norns, and the triune force of destiny, exemplified in the *Triune Maiden*, the Graces, the Muses, and The Erinyes. She is destiny, the avenger; the inspirer and the Beloved, ...Behold Her! She is She!

In this, they are revealed through their main virtues as Truth, Love and Beauty as the Triune Valkyries (Disir/Wyrd): *Idunna/Tyr (Urdhr) Frigga/Skogul(Skulde)* and *Freyja/Geiramul (Weorthunde)*, the bow/loom; shield/shuttle and spear/distaff give us the true meaning of the runes as a foundational matrix of creation; the boundary and sacred enclosure; the Holy Gardhr Tree; the Qutub and crossroads of sacrificial surrender. This describes perfectly the Creation of the Cosmos, its reflection upon the Earth as Edin, linked to the Heavens via the Asherah pole and Body of the Creatrix, and the point/place of Surrender through devotions given at the altar within the Holy of Holies – the Boundary of the Thing,[lxxxix] the Compass and Ring of Stones – The *Brisamingin* of Freyja.

These are what Roy Bowers enigmatically refers to as the *Necklace* – the ring of stones, of eight knots plus one more: ***the goddess comes from here!***

Skogul & Geiramul: two major ashwins, sister Norns being the spear and shield, the ravens Huggin and Munnin: From Old Norse *Geirr*, from *geirr/gar* (spear) (whence also*geir*).

Looking at the word Tyr as consonants, two/three runes express it:

- T = Irminsul. [victory in battle, but also symbol of the cremation/burial urns]
- yr is primal source/virtue... but then yr is also bow and *loom*!
- r is sun/shifting cycle/evolution.

Order of Being:

Tyr is the central core of the Norns, adjoined by Geiramul and Skogul: three primal forces active as the Fates, passive as Virtue within the Clan, and finally as Heritage. Tubal Cain and Namaah are the force and form of our known and named Tutelary deities via the ancestral current of lineage. They filter and represent the core qualities of the ineffable through the numerous and abstract gifts their mythologies bestow upon humankind.

Tubal Cain and Namaah remind us that our history in the sense of mystical ideologies and spiritual philosophies did not begin with Anglo-Saxon culture, but thousands of years earlier within a seething mass of diffusion, adoption appropriation and subsumation. They are each triune and reflect the Order of the Fates within the destinies of the People; they bring heaven to earth down the Tree to the Hearth below, within the *Thing,* the Grove and Nemeton of the People.

- ***Ida*** is the mythical homeland, the point of ancestral origin (Great-grandmother).
- ***Geiramul, Skogul & Tyr*** are Nordic names known to us for the Norns; each of them must have a presence in each world/level/ plane of being; the names of the Disir remain elusive at this time. Disir also control the flow of time and the destinies of all. Collective definition is to weave, entwine, envelop: i.e. the girdle/cord/net /loom etc. Saxon cognates are strongly suggested collectively as the Wyrd Sisters through *Iðunna/Tyr as Urdhr*; *Freyja/Geiramul as Weorthunde* and *Frigga/Skogul as Skulde.*
- ***Namaah & Tubal Cain*** are each the triune titular heads of the Clan Family representing the collective virtues of force and form, coalesced into a qualitative manifest expression and focal aspect within a quantifiable historical perspective. They are but two of the seven main tutelary beings [plus one]. The 8th spirit is that of Lucifer, the random Chaos of the North – Fenris -the hunter!
- ***Tyr, Geiramul & Skogul*** make presence too as winds within the 24 but are nevertheless aligned to Namaah. She is the active principle of wisdom, the Virtue/ Shakti, primal force just as Tubal is all generative form. Though the Fates rule all through the seven plus one forces, collectively there are more, around 24 plus one, plus one. They are known by the names remembered, by the deeds attributed to them and by the principles assigned to them.

T = Asgardhr [home of the gods]; third aett. Ruled by Tyr/ Zysa [Iðunna]

G = Midgardhr [home of humanity]; second aett. Ruled by Frigga/Rigg

S = Utgardhr [land of the dead and of shades]; first aett. Ruled by Freyja/Freyr

[The realm of transformation- Hella Herle/Herlequin, the dark one who complements the verdelet and leader of wild hunt].

Together these form the core, the main synthesis of the glyph through the names of Geiramul as the Spear, and Skogul as the Shield - the twin ashwins and companions to the third, Tyr, who holds the crown/rope/girdle/necklace and the light of 'Coma Berenice'; the glyph reveals this as 1734. One makes seven, makes three makes four: Gaud - Behold is She!

The Rainbow Bridge, Bi-Frost links all realms. Guarded by Heimdalhr/Rigg and Mordgud. It is not unreasonable to assume that Rigg is the precursor of Frigga?

Tyr as shining/resplendent *overseer* of order and justice, a clear cognate of Maat, holds fear and courage in balance when Fate decrees that defence is the only recourse to justice. As the bright Nowl star, Tyr/Tiwaz/Zeus /Zysa signifies the place of the Temple. This surely then infers the temple is overhead and below, following the erect shaft of the spear… as above so below? The temple is the blood acre that surrounds us….we are the conduit and receptacle for the overflowing of grace the mead poetry infuses.

Fate is higher than all gods. In acknowledging and naming Fate through their known forms we acquire some measure of understanding, listing a hierarchy of beings going back ever further and deeper.

The Idis/Disir [Valkyrie] are the prime agents of fate and the face of Fate is carried through Virtue. Through Fate, through our ancestral stream we return to the Mother, Ida, "*may she gather us up home again?*"

The boar, the deer, the ram we become!
For "the hunter and hunted are but one"

So to return to the question of **who** we are? We may now answer by the following definition:

The People *[existing now]* ***of*** *[bar]* ***Goda*** *[our ancestral mind/egregore],* ***of*** *[bar]* ***the Clan*** *[filial unit]* ***of Tubal Cain*** *[triune tutelary deity of innovation and evolution]!*

The 'Mothers' referred to so often by John and Roy are indeed the Fates, the triplicity, we now have names, identities and qualities for them. Ave! ***Urdhr, Weorthunde and Skulde***!

Historically, we hail from ***Ida,*** the ***Edin***, the ancestral homeland, source of manifest origin and of our humanity, the Grandmother wherein our root memory resides. This is retained and remains accessible through and by the ***Egregore*** [*the Goda*]. It is filtered and influenced by the tutelary being, named as ***Tubal Cain***, our promethean guiding spirit, under whose aegis we seek our way back, first of all to our point of origin , our homeland within the ancestral source [***Edin –Thule***] and finally, ultimately within the ineffable Source of All, She who is ***Providence*** and ***Paradise***. [***Ultima Thule***]. She is All Mothers and divine source of our spirituality.

Epilogue

Anyone entering the Stream must indeed be aware of the capacity in which they seek its activation. Understanding is everything. Indeed, it is something 'other' that validates who we are and what we do – be that a return to the source under anamnesis or through the gift of Egregore….the shift is within the spirit shadows on all planes. Where it alights there is no doubt, it is willed, imparted, inherited and achieved by merit, self-dedication and sacrifice to the spirit of Truth – that righteous causation of the stream's own vitality.

It is an organic process of ever-evolving gnosis unbound by fetters of dogma nourished by the Egregore, which *is* and must remain exclusive, dedicated to the preservation of the *core* within the stream in which it thrives. Others within that stream, or even skirting its peripheral borders, may also overlap at certain nodal intersections along the web of wyrd; they may partake of the essence but neither influence, stifle, nor develop it. Just as the Creator is not diminished by creation, the Source remains inviolate.

The letters written by Roy Bowers, once public, became exposed to compound views *not* consequent to the vital and express determinatives of that writer or recipient, bound within their original purpose and context of teacher/student dynamic. Wisdoms are imparted on many levels and keys earned along the way unlock new levels of seeing, according to the inbuilt parameters of relevant symbology applied to intrinsic Virtue – in this case of She who is codified by the inscrutable 'order of 1734.' Those not gifted with this core, will see it differently and thus evolve differently.

There are no secrets [regarding the esoteric mysteries] in the absolute sense, to those who hold the keys, hence declamations of such fall upon deaf ears... and yes, people do *make* secrets of information, views, actions, formulae and even common knowledge; moreover, these may even have value to others where revealed. But to hold these common things as secret is grossly manipulative.

No *Truth* is ever *Secret* and is therefore not the same at all as having no secrets. To maintain 'The Secret' is not to condone the withholding of information as secret; that should and could be given as aids to others whenever and wherever possible....what, where and to whom becomes part of the virtue holder's own lesson, to share and yet to hold, to discriminate and yet to yield....remembering always that *"Truth, no matter how we interpret it, feeds both the demon and the saint."*

Stasis, garnered by monitoring to whom and in what manner the stream is revealed, is the kiss of death. We can be led astray, so easily distracted by other paths that denude and cloud the clarity of our own – though these are not due to our own totems [who would always remain true to the core] leading us astray, but of similar totems belonging to other paths, to which we may relate at some level of our being. Keeping focused on our own is another part of the discipline attached to the core. The ego, ever one step ahead distracts us from the final prize, and keeps us chasing rainbows, when all the time, the gold resides within, requiring only *processing* – the 'Great Work.' Despite commonalities of 'tradition,' all must of necessity remain distinct. We may delight in those things we share, yet still, must respect and retain the points of divergence.

Whereas the real virtue holders need not be concerned by competing factions, because spout as they may, and claim what they will, spirit serves its own and will *not* work through them. Confidence in one's own point of 'Truth' requires no purpose then in engagement, argument or external validation. And though this may satisfy the virtue holder/s, and even those with whom they work or share it, or those who even 'recognize' it, others, seeking that core purity from afar may not appredend the Truth they cannot see. What we have we hold, but if kept hidden, then no one sees its light, the flame of Truth, of hope and illumination.

In honouring and protecting the gift of Virtue, we need not argue or fight for it. To say what is true and then uphold that in word and deed is sufficient. Hopefully, those who are able will see this; those who cannot, would not appreciate it with or without the fight. It is enough to announce the belief in one's own 'Truth.' To be silent, may *appear* noble and equally protective of its purity, but may in fact be perceived as a lack of conviction in one's worthiness.

North, North West, and North-East = Sentinels of the Mound;

One each beside Tubal and Namaah; one warrior under the aegis of Geburah through Mars & Saturn and the other a pilgrim under Chesed through Jupiter and Uranus. One is shin-yang to the other watery-yin, the primal abyss - the left and right hands of the Divil in the North. Hence the left banner is the graal and the right is the tau. The cross of Anu too, the solar cross of the cardinals constructs the two axes... a nebulous mystery older even than Tyr.. This divine all-force is Ing, possibly even Ing –Freyr. This force manipulates Space and Time, controls the winds, forming the arms of the swastika - the sacrificial being of force and form, the first matter…all potential, the motion of the stars around the point.

Tubal Cain as Master/Lord of this World/Matter, Anu/Cain as his progenitor as First Matter, Forming that which can be forged/refined by Tubal. Attachment generates permanence; but life is still important and what we do here is what sustains us beyond. But 'tis better to shelter in its vibrancy than outside its warmth in the cold ambivalence... that is how the Clan's worldview is its own and not anything other…we must be open to sense and feel fully, yet remain guarded, so that we filter for unwelcome intrusions we may deflect...and allow unhindered the all-pervading beauty of the light that burns the soul, otherwise we are but spectres in this place.

Three sons of Ptah, the great Geometrician, Grand Master Artificer, are generally known as Thoth, Djedi and Ham and are completely cognate with Tubal, Jubal and Jabal. On the issue of Qayin/Kain/Cain within our tradition, the ethos is not taken from the Old Testament texts, but from the earlier Sumerian texts upon which that story is based. There are numerous others that reveal earlier models for all the biblical major players. [i.e. Atrahasis as the original Noah etc.] We do not regard him to be the reaper of souls either, that mystery is fulfilled by another.

Our differences are theological, and in no way conflict with those at variance with them; traditions are founded upon distinct cosmologies, serving different eschatological needs, so require different mysteries to express them. CTC draws from a different pool to many, though we accept all as equally valid and profound.

Numerous debates exist in ancient texts between summer and winter, between plough and pickaxe, and one in particular, between cattle and grain related through two brothers named Emesh and Enten, who despite a violent quarrel are reconciled, all written circa 2,500BCE. These were clearly taken up by Jewish captives in Babylon in 6th century BCE and adapted to suite their own increasingly dualistic ethos expressing not inconsiderable angst as exiled people in captivity, railing bitterly against their perceived freedoms and loss of cultural and religious autonomy.

There is another factor to consider in this regarding the mistranslations of texts from original cuneiform to Hebraic, to Greek to Latin, to English…etc. whereupon one Hebrew scholar told me how the text does not actually state that Cain slew Abel at all,[xc] just that his hand was raised to his brother, for which dissent he was sent forth to fulfill another destiny; this dynamic is repeated in the Vedas, The Eddas, and so on. And can obviously be viewed literally or as a pedagogical analogy, for a host of Craft related allegories and their responsive mysteries.

Once an initial perspective is decided upon, praxis may be developed accordingly. It is agreed that Gnosticism did not survive as a practising faith, after the trials for heresy all but suppressed it, and before the Reformation outlawed even Catholicism to such an extent that no English monarch is allowed to hold that faith. It is now tolerated, but is deemed the *Old Religion.* For that reason its attendant superstitions, iconic idolatry etc. find favour still among those occultists desperate to cling to some measure of their praxis.

Much lore remains unraveled in the pages of that much-maligned Tome which preserve clues of an earlier, primal relationship, with the gods and the cosmos. The veneer and bias needs peeling, carefully, layer by layer, as in the restoration of an old painting. It has much to offer. Of course not all traditions world-wide are based in Judeo-Christian beliefs, but in England they mostly are, by default. It is and has been our culture for the best part of 1500 years.[xci]

Any occult systems developing within it will be based upon that premise. This is precisely why the 18th century Romantics sought a return to Arcadia, A pagan haven, free of such intrinsic bias implemented by the descent of prior cultural mores. The rest is history as they say. And the revival of many 'Craft' associated traditions during the 19th and 20th centuries were largely centralised around Judeo-Christian mythologies; a few only followed the pagan route, at least initially. The last few decades has further blended such original distinctions, allowing for the re-introduction of early pagan praxis and revivals. It must also be remembered that witchcraft has always existed within all religions, of whatever culture such practitioners are born unto. It is not the sole province of any religion having thrived under Christianity for many centuries before and since the 300 year Trials, instigated largely against Heresy – Gnosticism, the main branches of which are Cainite, Sethian and Johannite (Valentinian, would be the one flagged as closest to the Clan's enthos).

These would be worthy of study by any here intrigued by the notion of inclusion into cultic and occult praxes. One final though vital premise that holds yet another mystery regarding the word Cain, is how it is held by many scholars of etymology to be a 'loan' word, not of Jewish origin.

Chapter Fourteen

THE PEOPLE OF GODA: A PERSONAL HISTORY

Roy Bowers formed his second group known as the *Thames Valley Coven* which later changed its title become the *Royal Windsor Coven* retrospectively after Roy Bowers' own death in 1966. That is to say, during the time Roy Bowers was alive, it was not known by that name. John [EJJ] was under the impression this was likely to have been the influence of Marian Green when the *Regency* was formed as the outward expression of that group in order to better reflect its intent through a title complementary to that point of origin.

Bowers opened up this group around 1961/2 after his former group collapsed due to differences of opinion. Over time he gradually drafted in various seasoned crafters such as Ronald White and George Winter. Madge Worthington and her then partner MG, joined the troupe as did John Jones and his wife Val; Doreen Valiente, along with Bill & Bobbie Gray who followed much later around 1964. Marion Green did not attain full membership and was in fact only with them for a very short time. Many guests came and went, including Norman Gills, Gerard Noel and others, attending odd Rites here and there.

"The idea was aired that a more democratic order should be developed, loosening the standard 'cuveen' structure and its attendant hierarchies. This was the beginning of the Clan proper. Roy effectively remained it Magister and head, although after his death, when the Regency continued but few of the works of the Clan's, this position was deemed null and void. However, E. J. Jones, Val Jones and Jane Bowers continued the Clan of Tubal Cain and its entire works."

When writing to Bill [William Gray] once, Roy Bowers mentioned the Sword and broom Mystery, illustrated with a diagram of the six pointed star imposed upon a head, upper-point over the Ajna chakra and lower point over the Vishuddi chakra. Again, like the Mask blessing this closely resembles a covering of the sensory organs in between these two points that transform thought into the work and communicate wisdom drawn thereof.

Another larger illustration transposes this same six pointed pattern to the compass round within a ditch of water, broom socketed brush uppermost, upright, central to the circular trench around it. Many of the Rites feature both Water and Fire, in fact fire, beneath the Cauldron was considered the creative spark infusing the contents with inspiration, carried through the air as steam.

All knives plunged into the seething liquid, would draw concentrated drops to hallow the Compass itself. In the Compass of Roy Bowers, we have the Triad of Life – Birth/Death/Rebirth. This expands to the Pentagram Round of Life – Birth, Youth/Initiation, Love/Wisdom /Death/Peace. Initiation and Peace were those qualities used by Robert Graves in his excellent work on the Greek Myths. Roy Bowers substituted them for those of Youth and Death to better illustrate his visionary mythos.

The Greek smith Hephaestus, whom is likened often to Tubal Cain, has an interesting structure to his name. When broken down to two Greek forms, it becomes:

Hemer – phaistos = '*he who shines by day*'

Similarly, Gwenevere becomes:

Gwen/Evo Gwen/Eve = '*first woman and (pale) queen*'

In Numerology, the four-letters that represent God, given as YHVH is linked to ea; VO; ay; known better as EVA!

Adam, the first man.

As King of the World, this phrase breaks down to support this as the earth, and its king.

K = ruler, the rune for light and *kain* and *ing* is of course the earth itself, the divine god that permeates it. But in point of fact, as a derivative of queen, *k-ing* holds his virtue from her.

Chapter Fifteen

A Pellar's Fate: The Legacy of the *'People of Goda, of Clan Tubal Cain'*

1. The Round of Life: Death

I know that I hung on a windy tree
nine long nights,
wounded with a spear, dedicated to Odin,
myself to myself,
on that tree of which no man knows
from where its roots run.[xcii]

On Midsummer's Eve 1966, Roy Leonard Bowers consumed a fatal cocktail of herbs and prescription medicines, collapsing into a coma. He died nine days later in hospital without regaining consciousness. Invoking the 'faerie rade,' he sought an audience with Madame la Guiden; thereto seek a 'trial' in which he might resolve his fate.[xciii] His controversial suicide forty-six years ago has raised many theories regarding his involvement within the Craft as one of its most gifted exponents. The facts reveal the torment of frustrated genius and anarchy within the mind of this tragic poet, who'd dared to eat from the table of the gods.

Inspired and intoxicated by Odhin's honeyed mead, sacred manna to his ravenous soul, his life turned sour through strife, a gift from Eris whose bitter herbs peppered his dish too often, inflaming his innate sense of injustice. Nonetheless, precious moments of grace imparted glimpses to him of the philosopher's stone, of wisdom's fruit, the gift of his undeniable genius, manifest as immortal, perennial philosophy within his work and the stream that flows steadily from it and serves it still.

Through considered exploration of all influences brought to bear upon Roy Bowers and his contemporaries, we might better see the man through his works. During the phenomenon of the 'swinging sixties,' a huge groundswell of philosophy, spiritualism, astro-sciences, political anarchy together with new and greater freedoms of religion and occult practice, collectively nurtured the context in which Roy Bowers was fashioned into the forthright seeker of answers believed to be within his reach. Intensely charismatic and self-assured, his seductive charm drew both men and women into his company.

When Doreen Valiente eventually met him in 1964, she could not help but describe him as 'strikingly handsome.[xciv] Undeniably arrogant and opinionated, it is clear this was tolerated only when it served the best intentions of his peers within the Craft, a trial that became increasingly impossible as tolerance collapsed into a quagmire of delusion; his increasing provocations accelerated his eventual alienation from all but his closest friends.

Without question this exemplary figure possessed a keen sense of the presence of the 'other,' a magnetic talent that drew many to gravitate within his orbit. A natural leader, Roy Bowers was a trendsetter, a 'mover and shaker,' whose innovations still resound within the occult world to this day. One distinguishing tenet, unprecedented in his time, was of belonging to a stream of traditions contra to extent ideologies of Wicca as presented by Gerald B. Gardner.

To underscore this, Roy Bowers described himself thus:

"I describe myself as a Pellar. The People are formed in Clans or families and they describe themselves by the local name of the Deity. I am a member of the People of Goda - of the Clan of Tubal Cain. We were known locally as 'witches', the 'Good People'. Green Gowns' (females only) 'Horsemen' and finally as 'Wizards'."

It is apparent that one title he'd chosen not to use, infers that 'witch' is not a title proclaimed of oneself but one employed by others, with regard to the nature of the work engaged:

'What do witches call themselves? They call themselves by the name of their Gods. I am Od's man, since the spirit of Od lives in me.

And, even more explicit, he expands upon that by saying:

"Now, what do I call myself? I don't. Witch is as good as any; failing that 'Fool' might be a better word. I am a child of Tubal Cain, the Hairy One."

To quantify those remarks, Roy Bowers then feels it necessary to expound 'wisdom' as the lure:

".... since talking about the People (we describe ourselves as such) ....The religion is even more mystical than most - so words are very poor approximations of what we actually discover or feel about our beliefs......so we come to the heart of the People, a belief that is based upon eternity, and not social needs or pressures - the 'witch' belief then is concerned with Wisdom, our name is The People and Wisdom is our aim."

Bowers however, bemoaned the lack of good apprentices, of unworthy masters, of superficial groups and media hype. He stated more than once between the group's inception in 1961 to its decimation in 1966 that he wished to leave his group behind and work alone, that they held him back and that he was weary of struggling to maintain his authority and weary of their failure to understand his vision. Thus he became progressively more unreasonable, prone to consistent deepening melancholia. Frustrated and vengeful, he chose to focus on a more spiritual 'Truth' gained through the arduous pathway of the Mysteries.

"I am master of a small clan, the devil in fact. I in turn recognise the authority of those who are higher than myself, and that authority, once stated, is absolute, do what we may."

He speaks here of the Law, of its responsibilities and duties; He makes a clear comment regarding his position, his perception of the honour they accumulate. His expression of 'Truth' has also become subject to much recent debate with his detractors denouncing his system of belief as disruptive and prone to chaos. As heir to his work, I would refute that unmitigatedly, and yet it is certain that elements of 'mystery' reside unresolved, a reminder perhaps that the 'Old Master' is no longer here in the flesh to keep 'order.'

Focus begins upon the 'arte' with the journeymen's argosy to discover their own evolution of spirit through the 'gnostic' legacy intrinsic to this stream. Both Gerald B. Gardner and Roy Bowers ardently promoted their occult philosophies as bound within 'religion' and yet, much to the chagrin of both founders, this fundamental tenet of their belief has been rejected by many of their practitioners. Forty years later, the 'Craft' remains as divisive as ever. Bowers declared Truth to be the one constant within all realms where illusion obfuscates the goal. He asserted that the Ancient Mysteries, whilst not being secret, hold the means by which man may come to know himself and God, which is again the Highest and most sacred Truth.

Witchcraft and paganism had always maintained a discreet presence within orthodoxy, being contra to the freedoms afforded by modern Wicca. And so we certainly need to promote the vast range within the Craft in order to admonish the popular stereotypical image of it. This gave serious impetus to an objective that abides to the caveat that unlike Roy, I do not believe the Craft should be termed a 'religion' for many reasons including proscriptive dogma and predominantly extreme intolerances that negate all things of a deeply spiritual nature. So whereas the term ‘religious’ was used indiscriminately by Bowers, I think perhaps in order to inspire deeper connections within the ‘Craft’ he believed the Craft too detrimentally obsessed with spell-work.

Bowers advocated how the measure of each seeker lay in their ability to rout falsity as a harmonic of devout ‘acts of glorious wonder’ preferably factored into their praxes. Each person works alone on this path, even within the Clan. It was the primary concern of Evan John Jones, for everyone down the line to avoid the traps of Fate Bowers subjected himself too. Prejudice ate into the very soul of Roy Bowers, poisoning his rationale until he saw ‘witch-hunters’ behind every active political campaign or policy. But is not Ma'at also Cosmic Truth, higher than our mortal perceptions, and does not Her wisdom enflame us all to higher principles? Each of us must take up the tools of the smith and forge our own destiny, preserve our own honour and destroy and release that which does not serve our evolution in Truth, Love and Beauty.

Correspondences between Bowers and others may occasionally turn up over the next few years revealing ever more about this unique individual and of the Craft he devoted his life to, particularly with regard to his intentionally oblique identity, tempered later through his mystical shift. Certainly the two recent letters discovered in a cache to Robert Graves reveal a political, vulnerable and somewhat cynical man, cleverly 'fishing' a known authority on mythology, testing the waters.

Enquiring, yet cajoling of Graves, their value is revealed as the key to his great legacy. Throughout his numerous published works[xcv] Roy shrouds his early life in mystery, alluding occasionally to his own desolation in his enforced denial of what he called the teachings of the blood, until his late teens. Picking up the colourful threads of his life, he weaves his experiences gained in the occult field during his work in a foundry and on the canals; both close knit repositories of folklore and alternative beliefs.

Bowers expounded a lineage spanning five generations, highlighting where his great-grandfather once reigned as 'Grand Master of the Staffordshire Witches,' and of his father being a Horse Whisperer. He further claimed that his own mother had been the Maid and scryer for an old local coven in Windsor during the reign of Queen Victoria, that two unnamed ancestors had been hung for witchcraft, and finally, that in childhood, Diana, had 'plucked' him for Her own.[xcvi]

Another, and no less profound experience of the Horned God, a brooding, dark and vetivert scented form 'as old as time,' left a lasting impression upon him. Fact or Faith? Professor Ronald Hutton of Bristol University after careful study of his work, stated: 'he was either 'genuine or genius.'[xcvii] Such opinion remains fundamental to the current and wave of influence absorbed by all those touched by its flow. His light was the sharpness, the clarity of vision that invigorated and illuminated all the disparate shards and fragments of lore he hungrily consumed along the trail of his own tragic argosy.

Around November 1963 he began writing a spate of articles for occult magazines, first 'Psychic News', with 'Genuine Witchcraft is Defended,' with others appearing in 'New Dimensions.' Then, later in 1964 after the death of Gerald B. Gardner, four more pieces were penned for 'The Pentagram.' Here he became involved in some very unsavoury polemics along with his associate 'Taliesin' against Arnold Crowther, a well known witch of the Sheffield Coven and husband to Patricia Crowther and High Priestess of Gardnerian Craft, both of whom had known Gardner very well. Somewhat harshly, he promoted the concept of what he termed 'grey magic' which allowed him to expertly weave yarns into circumstance, leaving the recipient bewildered and uncertain about where the boundaries of fact and fiction began and ended.

In fact he was not beyond pulling off a major 'hoax,' a regrettable scenario the author Enid Corral (aka Justine Glass) was subject to with regard to an incident involving a Copper plate that he allegedly attempted to pass off as a family heirloom; in another discussion he gave her his interpretation of symbols carved upon a French Menhir. His undisputed negative comments about her was in fact less concerned with her believing the information regarding the symbols on the stone, (as he understood them, they are actually correct) and more concerned with her lack of interest in researching them beyond their face value. Her superficial attitude inculcated his contempt. Both the plate and monolith were later featured within her book.[xcviii]

Nonetheless, he was a flawed anti-hero, untypical and revolutionary. Being a thoroughbred non-conformist was never going to win him the approval of the middle-class establishment he despised and held in disdain. His scathing candour and propensity to mock these 'good' folk of the fashionable set, who take tea, have sherry and cake, who sought only the flaccid rudiments of his passion were to him, less than approachable, less than tolerable, and yet, he did, in spite of himself garner their good graces. With gritted teeth he attended cocktail parties, book launches, gallery viewings all with an eye to being perceived well for his innovative views or be scorned for their lack of vision.

And yet he attracted a number of known and respected occultists to work with him. Clearly he radiated a profound sense of the other detectable and tangible to all who met him; in fact without exception, they all record a most remarkable vibrancy and luminosity about him.[xcix] Having an empathic awareness of this, he utilised it to great effect, manipulating those around him towards his vision. Working outside, in what would now be deemed as shamanically, he kept the ritual form close to his chest. In effect, he became the 'Supreme Master of Ceremonies,' orchestrating each musician to their finest tune. To date, none of those who worked with Roy Bowers, or who had been present at one of his rituals has since found its measure. Leading his Clan, a 'magical group based along the seven and one basis,'[c] he declared himself its trickster and master - the 'devil' explaining that the occult truth mirrored the outer plane where the Creatrix reigns supreme upon the inner plane. Choosing dramatic locations, high on hill tops, open to the winds, his many haunts and working sites included:

"Burnham Beeches in Berkshire, Witney Clumps in Oxfordshire, the Sussex Downs, Cheddar Gorge in Somerset and the Brecon Beacons in South Wales. Black and hooded robes were worn and power was raised by pacing or dancing in a circle around a central fire. The ritual tools used included a knife, a cord, a stone, a cauldron, a human skull, a cup or drinking horn and a forked staff called a Stang."[ci]

Fairly early on in the group, an old guy from Westmoreland (could have been early correspondence with Bill Gray), provided him with considerable occult and craft information. Then in Letter iv to Bill, he describes the new people coming in as the "basis of a working group at last – factory workers, rough diamonds, school teachers, an artist and a mechanical genius." These clearly refer to John, Chalky and George. He adds how they were discovered by his two apprentices (unknown but possibly Arthur and his Diana). Doreen Valiente was also writing to him at this time.

Numerous sources fed into and nourished the 'Clan of Tubal Cain,' advancing its development exponentially from the Clan's original foundation as the 'Thames Valley Coven,' particularly with regard to their wide-ranging knowledge and experiences, severally and collectively. Evan John Jones brought the threads of 'The Rose Beyond the Grave,' amongst other curious lore and George 'Winter' donated threads of the 'Cave and the Cauldron Rite' assisting its creation and eventual formulation.[cii] Certain rites and methods of working along with codes and law were constructed in adherence to even older formulae known to Ronald White and others, bound together under the guiding light of Roy Bowers. They marked their working area with ash and soot, but not as a boundary, rather it delineated the main area to be used for ease, to keep all participants together. Sabbat fayre was also traditional, consisting of easily transportable foods such as bread, meat, cheese, butter, apples and wine.

To all guests and outsiders it appeared their intent focused upon the Horned God, when in fact it was the divine, fair Diana, who received adoration from her darling crew. The Horned One, the presence in the Stang, was also the guardian of the dancing floor, the bridge and link between realms as the Lord of the Dance Himself! Calendrical rites reflect Christianised folklore in the round of celebrations and observances called knots by the Clan, including telling the maze; the skull and mound; crossing the Lethe; adding to the glamour and beguilement of those seekers of esoteric keys within this stream.

Most of all Bowers was keen to assert theological differences between his perception of genuine witchcraft and paganism, despite an obvious overlap in their pathways into the Mysteries, elevating his work beyond the presumed stasis of these seeming primitivisms, through a heady trance-inducing mix that he insisted distinguished his work from those: "pagans, being naught but dancing peasants." Eschatological and cosmological principles were factored into the Mythos gleaned from inspired, visionary experiences based within their collective traditions, becoming increasingly modeled upon philosophical and heavy theological truisms, through the well-spring of company and the 'work.'

In general practice, multiple fires were prepared within two or three designated areas, where the workings would occur, open to the wind and all elements. The Clan's Tutelary deity presides over the civilising arts of music, poetry and agriculture and is shadowed by his tanist twin, the psychopompic god of death, together forming the complex composite - the divine smith, Tubal Cain.[ciii] Pale Leukathea, the cold, ambivalent yet ruthless 'femme fatale' is Supreme Mistress of the Fates, sirens, harpies, but also the graces, and is ultimately, 'Truth.' Manifest through 'Wyrd.' Her hidden aspect is Nox the dark wisdom goddess, from whom is drawn the 'child of compassion,' the illuminator and guide to mankind. Adhering strongly to the Anglo-Saxon tradition, She commands the Northern point of the Compass from where deceased souls taken by Her wild geese fly hither upon the bitter winds in Her train. Another tenet of this particular stream of the Traditional Craft concerns the compassion of Prometheus who invites the wrath of Nemesis upon himself for choosing to advance mankind. Such deeply considered comprehensions were to Bowers, profound truths upon which his die was cast.

"I am pain, grief, sorrow and tears, The rack, noose and stake.
The flayer and the flayed, The hunted and the hunter.
The Head without a body, Thrust upon a stake.
The body without a head, Hung upon a tree/
Yea! All this, but still am whole."[xciv]

But Roy was fated to die alone, perplexed, bereft of his grand title, a recluse at odds with himself and the world. Having fallen foul of his ego-driven dictatorial manner, his friends and family abandoned him, one by one. Feeling without hope of achieving his destiny in this life, he made his gambit, exploiting his belief in re-incarnation, wherein the Pale Faced Goddess would return him once again to his fold to complete the work he'd failed to fulfill in that carnated form. In one of his many letters to myself, John, writing in august 2000, cautioned us regarding commitment to a magical path:

"Once you embrace a dedicated magical path, you must live within its bounds and mythos; to forget that mundane and profane are one, to step out from its boundaries, is to invite chaos."[xcv]

2. Birth: The Emergence of Hope

The death of a leader is an inconsolable loss. Invariably, factionalisation and despair are consequential to bereavement. Restoration of equilibrium is seldom swift and the interim often generates its own problems as attempts to deal with the grievous issue of trauma induced events connected to that death. From within the 'Cuveen' previously led by Roy Bowers a previously concealed archive of material finally opens a window into the workings of a modest group that, according to a document dated 1961, named the: 'Writ and Constitution.' [cvi] It reveals and confirms the former name of the group as being 'The Thames Valley Coven.' That this document has survived the passage of time is testament to the tenacity of the spirit of those strong men whose visionary ideals are preserved for all to study in their original pioneering context.

Since the 1980s though, persistent rumour has advanced the suggestion that the 'Thames Valley Coven' became the 'Royal Windsor Coven' in Roy Bowers' own lifetime.

Though fascinating and seductive in light of persistent rumour circulated by others since both the deaths of both Roy Bowers and Evan John Jones, the idea must remain one of speculation awaiting further information for its support. Sadly neither of those men are here to dispute these claims, which rest upon a crossed out typed title on a page in biro, written over with a pen with RWC replacing TVC. There is of course no way to date that amendment to the original typed document.

But this very much detracts from the very real importance of the jewel revealed here, of his actual working group, hitherto unknown. In point of fact Roy's widow denied their coven ever being named the RWC, and John likewise, who added his view that certain people from the USA, conspired with others here in the UK to circulate this as fact. Their motives remain unclear though John remained convinced it was to disguise its true origin. In truth, we may never know, and to ponder on this, loses the real importance of this and other documents within this archive.

In a letter to Bill Gray [cvii] dated circa 1963, Roy refers to himself as the Master of a small 'Coven.' A similar statement is announced in a letter to Joe Wilson in which Roy describes himself to be aged 35 and a member of the 'People.' This has further confirmation in another earlier letter written to Ronald (Chalky) White, an elder of that coven.

Within this document, Roy imposes his authority as leader as he issues to them directives and instruction for works being formulated.[cviii] Intriguingly, Roy refers to his wife as 'High Priestess' in this early document, suggesting immaturity of Craft terminology at a formative stage of this fledgling group. Falling back on a 'Wiccan' model (known to all of them) admits an absence of familiarity with Craft[cix]. Clearly, at this point, both he and Jane were still 'finding their way.' Another missive relates his pathological drive to announce his knowledge to the world, where reined in by others of the group and unable to run with his inspiration and increasing experience, he expresses his frustration. He bemoans of them:

" ... although in some ways I have power over them, they also have power over me, and this is one of their decisions."

Eventually, this all changed dramatically under the curious influence of the 'Old man from 'Westmoreland,' a man described by Bowers as: "being born inside the pale of the faith who claims hereditary knowledge…" Of the Long Compton folk he says little, except to assert they had taught him much, including the secret of the wand and stone. Writing to yet another 'old boy,' he shared generously of his knowledge with Norman Gills, boasting to him of his wife, his property and his craft legacy.

Gills brought to the group his friendship and much cunning lore, becoming a fond and frequent guest. Evan John Jones later joined these merry men in early 1963. One George Winter is the focus of another document where instructions are given to modify and adapt his own induction rite.[cx] At that time the Coven consisted of five others, Roy and his wife, the later Maid of the Clan, 'Arthur' and his good 'Lady,' and last but not least, Ronald White.

These events are noteworthy, for their relativity to the events following Roy's death in 1966. Effectively the group split into two; Ronald, George, Norman Gills and Marion Green formed one group of like mind; Roy's widow, John and his good lady formed a second and tightly distinct group. Doreen along with Bill and Bobbie Gray remained friendly to both groups, having contact until their individual deaths. Expanding on this, Doreen delivers an afterthought in her summary of this tragedy, whereby she states that it was Jane who held the real power of the Clan.[cxi] However, both groups honoured their original stream of admission, transferring only that arcane lore into their praxis, once formerly their own.

Both groups built upon the same foundation sourced from the coven headed by Roy and Jane as Magister and Maid irrespective of its title of Royal Windsor or Thames Valley, each then cultivated their diverse individuality with considerable depth and passion of execution: One as The Clan of Tubal Cain in continuance, albeit under new guardianship developing the triune male, female and priestly mysteries centred upon the Stang. The other as the Regency emerged as an exoteric form of the RWC that focused on sacred kingship, natural mysticism and the folkloric seasonal round. Both continued to honour the Young and Old Horn King, The Divine Feminine (Diana – Pale Leukathea) observing the tenets of Fate, Truth, Love and Beauty. The enduring Mythos of the Rose Castle, the heart of the pentagramatic compass rose sourced and vitalised both groups, the virtue of which CTC maintain still. The manifest Compass is a reflection of it celestial counterpart.

"Red and flaming is the Fire
Within that Hall of the High Queen.
Filled with bright wine is the bowl in Her hand,
Her eyes are blue and shining as the sea.
How many shall go therein and return?"[cxii]

And so it now falls to myself to complete the course with an overview of Clanship, especially relative to the 'People of Goda, of the Clan of Tubal Cain.' Clan is a very specific term that determines a group of people united by an actual or perceived ancestor. Kinship is acknowledged through birth or adoption into this group and although this system is not strictly hierarchical, the head kinsman rules. All are bound together in troth to a specific henotheistic deity; in this case Tubal Cain. Throughout his few published letters, Roy Bowers occasionally made note of the Clan system, of the three groups within his Clan dedicated to maintain the sites and rituals of the three mysteries of the priesthood (the 'Godhi) the Clan is predicated upon.[cxiii] E.J. Jones discusses this in his book 'Sacred Mask Sacred Dance.'[cxiv]

"The hardest thing of all is coming to terms with and accepting the overwhelming all embracing totality of the godhead trying to reduce it to mere simple terms and the one that Cochrane gave us, likened the godhead to a multi faceted jewel, of which we see only one face. So to Cochrane and those of us who are members of the People of Goda of the Clan of Tubal Cain, the godhead is always expressed in terms of the goddess, the mother of all creation and the giver of life and death." [cxv]

3. Love: Realisation of Truth

"When the shadow faces from the past draw close, and claim you for their own, You drift through past lives and places my friend, to seek the Castle and the Rose."[cxvi]

Believing that 'Truth' is variable, and that 'what is true today will be not be tomorrow' even our memories defeat us, locked in a distant moment when those elements were true only in that context. My first impression of John (E.J. Jones) is nonetheless one I shall never forget. Somewhat jaded by the incredible fugue of a punishingly fierce heat wave, I had alighted the train and ambled wearily into a seething mass of shoppers and travellers. Peering around I spotted John; He lifted his head to catch my gaze in an eerie moment of mutual recognition.

By the time of John's death in August 2003, seven fruitful but intense years later, blessings of weal and woe had befallen us through his often difficult but invaluable friendship, each a constant boon and source of frustration to both myself and Robin, my partner and Magister of the Clan. Subject to John's austere guidance during our numerous visits to his home, we grasped the imperative rudimentary elements of our Craft. John's mentorship, though exacting and bewildering, proved enormously beneficent as he deftly juggled the roles of tutor, friend and guide; joking frequently that Robert Cochrane had named him – 'the worst witch in the world.' Like Roy, John had been a belligerent devotee to the Pale Faced Goddess or 'Diana.' Having surrendered himself to Her, he cautioned us that:

"Once you embrace a dedicated magical path, you must live within its bounds; to forget that mundane and profane are one, to step out from its boundaries, is to invite chaos."[cxvii]

Gregarious and astute, this man was not one easily fooled, although he loved to play that role himself. Being 'Old School' he was an exacting task master, tough and unstinting in his expectations. He saw 'glamour' and 'grey magic' as unnecessary distractions, a hangover from a more superstitious time, preferring instead a more direct and uncompromising expression of belief and practise. In fact, when we once asked his advice on a problem we were experiencing, he responded with:

"no sense in wasting time and energy on spell craft or magic when a punch in the mouth works just as well."

This was indeed his perennial philosophy; if it could be dealt with easily then it should be. Matters of the mundane and of this realm should be dealt with in appropriate and relative manner; he asserted that magic belonged only to the realms of spirit. His wisdoms regarding detachment have stayed with me and there is not a day passes that I am not aware of his voice guiding me in my thoughts or actions. Of the man himself, we may reveal that it was John's impression that his line of blood lay with either the 'Silures' or the 'Demetae;' both tribes had in fact been based across the border in Wales close to his family village. Later, his involvement in the Craft began slowly as a gradual process from his youthful encounter through friendship with another whose family held considerable farmland in West Wycombe (Buckinghamshire). This led to his adoption into their tradition centred around a Horned Deity, then to his eventual and fateful meeting with Roy Bowers. During Evan John Jones' valuable time with the people of Wycombe, he absorbed a not inconsiderable amount of lore that became acutely significant to the volatile and impressionable Roy Bowers.

With Roy Bowers and his wife, he formed a firm and lasting friendship, enduring many issues of ego, pride, folly and sorrow. Evan John Jones quickly became inducted into the 'Clan of Tubal Cain' around 1963 meeting several other crafters Roy had attracted to its core a couple of years earlier around 1961.[cxviii] Others of note soon followed. The Craft scene, though one he purposely steered clear of, was at that time very small and almost everyone knew or knew of everyone else in it. Despite his familiarity amongst a rich variety of occultists from diverse practises, John firmly believed that there was common ground between all of them. John had borne the role of 'Man in Black' within the 'Clan of Tubal Cain,' assuming only later the Magisterial post when Roy's own widow and Maid bequeathed John the mantle along with its 'Virtue' and full responsibility following the tragic death of Roy Bowers in 1966, its former Magister and founder of the Tradition in this form.

Holding the tradition for many years after, John continued to work its mysteries alongside those of other traditions he encountered among his friends and acquaintances, especially William Gray and Doreen Valiente with whom he developed a considerable Craft relationship. Tutor and mentor to numerous correspondents, his advice and opinion became much sought after among his notable peers, including Nigel Jackson, Andrew Chumbley, Joseph 'Bearwalker' Wilson, Stuart Inman, Tony Steel, Iain Steele and Caroline Tully, drawing enquiries from as far afield as North and South America, Australia, Africa and Eurasia. Many other anonymous names and faces consulted and received advice from this gregarious bear of a man. Unlike his predecessor, Roy Bowers, John believed that the Craft could be of value to those Roy would never have considered as being 'of the blood' (in the literal sense).

Perhaps somewhat ironically, John is best known for his adoption into the Clan of Tubal Cain, certain people from America, well known personages from an offshoot of the '1734' System and Method of employing traditional means to pursue the mysteries. These people in America however had sought advancement within each element of the original flux that generated it.[cxix] In that regard, John had unwittingly exposed himself to pointless controversy, eventually seeking a means of correction via familiar media open to him. His private papers refute utterly their contra claims and his final interview with Mike Howard editor of the occult magazine, 'The Cauldron'[cxx] just weeks before his death, publically cleared all concerns and doubts of those uncertain of his direction and motivations. This was very much clarified and supported by facts asserted within John's final book: 'The Robert Cochrane Letters' co-authored by Mike Howard. He was up to his last breath a devoted child of the goddess, 'plucked by Diana as one of her darling crew' as oft he would say, somewhat wistfully. Every Full Moon he would raise a cup to Her where again he strongly believed that one could satisfactorily work alone and in his very first letter to me he advised me that:

"The hardest thing of all for people to grasp is that no-one actually needs a group to become a 'witch,' witch is only a name, there are no degrees of initiation to go through or anything like that. You find what you want and develop it yourself and this will have as much validity in the eyes of the goddess as any formal gathering."[cxxi]

In fact this neatly sums up his nature in embracing his Craft, which was his life - fluid, adaptable, flexible, dedicated, earnest, sincere and versatile. He was also pragmatic and headstrong, broken only by his outrageous humour bordered on the cheeky, being full of 'schoolboy' fun. If there was a 'dark' side to John, it was his absolute uncompromising brevity in his approach to the 'work'...he was all for fun before and after the event – but the work was deadly serious. He did not suffer fools easily and hid his contempt well from those he considered unworthy; being a gentleman, his manners overrode much his instinct yelled out to acknowledge. John added in a later letter:

"In fact, in the beginning, when working with Cochrane, we were actually practising a rather basic form of the old shamanistic witchcraft without realising it; at the same time, no-one had ever thought of putting it into a more formal footing......the deeper you go into this, the more you realise that the craft is not the be all and end all, so that in the end, you stop being a witch and become a magus, a magician in the old sense of the word."[cxxii]

Right from the beginning recorded in his next letter was his absolute conviction that we;

"all, sooner or later find what we need rather than what we want."[cxxiii]

And yet he would also refer to himself as 'Od's man. He was certainly a man of complex and seeming contradiction, yet also an eternal optimist, harbouring no regrets, despite the difficult hurdles life forced him to face. Many long nights we would burn the midnight oil, philosophising over all manner of topics relating to the mundane and sacred worlds. When speaking once of Fate and its importance within the Clan's Mythos, I proffered how we have no 'free will' as the 'Three Ladies' have long woven their weft of time and space? To which he simply assured me: "we have to live out our 'Fate/Doom." That was my first lesson in the 'Web of Wyrd.'

Most intriguing of all was the Stag, a symbol of Kingship, divine authority, and psychopomp – a true leader of his kin. Being John's totem, it had become represented through his own Stag mask. [cxxiv] He poignantly removed this small metal icon from between the tangs of the staff in passing it over to me, so that the Magister that followed him could place his own totem where his had previously reigned. He told me of Roy's, and I remember thinking what a profound thread this had spun, a legacy as told through totems, particularly as Roy had made John his spiritual heir long before his tragic death in 1966. What made this even more poignant was the realisation that the shaft of the Magister's Hand staff had been formed from the haft section of Roy's own Staff.

The Stang was referred to by John as 'the child of wisdom' and the middle pillar or Yggdrassil, the world tree upon which Odhin hangs entranced, listening to the wind whispering Her wisdoms there even as the Mother embraces him in Her thrall. Thus She bears him upon Herself, the Stang, symbol of the divine 'Tree of Life.' She is both Serpent and Eve; He is both Adam and Cain. This is why John was so insistent that the Maid and no other 'holds' the Stang, for whosoever wields it, raises Cain. There was an old occult maxim John was rather fond of concerning 'truth' where:

"The male head of the Clan reflects the occult truth that this world is a mirror image of the inner plane, in which this world is his [as Her representative] and the other world is Hers."

Moreover, John believed that a Magister should and must therefore be in full accord with that role as just and true guardian, especially in the sense of one untainted by error. His extreme sense of honour and justice permeated his view that only by embracing these principles into oneself could one generate evolutionary growth and progression onto a higher path:

"He who wields Odhin's spear never fails to hit the mark."[cxxv]

When speaking of curses and cursing, ethics in that regard and certain myths and fables, he had responded somewhat perplexedly to first mark the law, then to consider how:

"The curse of Ol' Tubal lies in the management of the Clan itself. You are stuck with it until you feel the need to download it on someone else and when you do, you'll get a tremendous feeling of lightness and relief. In the end you find if you let it, it will rule your entire life and that quite simply is, the 'curse.[cxxvi]

This comment was his response to a question I had asked him concerning the well known 'curse of Cain.' He did add the remark that though the mantle was heavy, it could also be a blessing at best. It was simply a paradox. His philosophy regarding life is one many might consider harsh, even brutal; in fact his pragmatic minimalism cut through all aspects of his life. In fact he strongly believed that we must all bear our conviction inwardly asserting that:

"you do not have to justify your work to anyone – this is how we work, and this is what we believe in, and it is no-one else's business. They either accept that or they do not, as must you."[cxxvii]

John was keen to promote the gnostic premise that asserts each person must tread their own path and not walk in the steps of another. No journey may be duplicated, no information relevant, irrespective of who they are. So this man's work, being his own and relevant only to his process of gnosis would not best serve another, and must be destroyed lest it present an impediment to another's process of gnosis. Having forged my own path, I am obliged to concur with this principle; no-one may grasp another's insights. But he did sustain, enflesh and honour the priceless legacy for those who follow him; and in this, for reader's of 'The White Goddess' by Robert Graves,' he played his part as the 'Roebuck' to the very end.

4. Maturity: Peace Through Realization

Roy's charismatic nature had drawn people to him like moths to a flame. Gravitating to his undeniable magnetism they were paradoxically as quickly repelled by his bigoted intolerances. His drive to coerce them into a competent unit, compatible and able to face the 'other' generated one of several surviving documents, revealing his hitherto undiscovered talent for missives, shepherding his flock, refining and redefining their purpose and goals within the Clan.

One of these missives, entitled, 'Beliefs and Practises'[cxxviii] expresses his concerns that independence was undermining the development of the 'Egregore.' He opens the letter with:

"To all Elders, the real fault at the heart of the group seems to be a lack of understanding of these basic principles. As long as this misunderstanding continues, we cannot create a 'group mind', therefore we cannot expect to work a 'group magic', irrespective of our [own] powers."

E. J. Jones developed further the rites frequently alluded to by Bowers as his explanation of the Male and Female Mysteries of the Clan of Tubal Cain. Specifically, they both mention the division of The Clan of Tubal Cain into holders of the Male and Female Mysteries headed by The Maid and The Magister respectively. A third section of the Faith that encapsulated the Priestly Mysteries to which some believe Roy Bowers to have inferred had been lost 'a long time ago.' E. J. Jones maintained this was simply Roy's bemoaning of an acute lack of spirituality within Craft practices extant during their own era, such that their recovery would present an arduous and grueling Quest. In actuality, it was the female mysteries that had been missing, as we eventually discovered, after chasing several lapwings.

In order to avoid confusion between these Triune Mysteries and (the three) working sites relevant to the Priestly Mysteries alone, E.J. Jones clarifies this querulous issue further by discussing Bowers' belief that some of the old Traditional Clans (including his own) had once been large enough to allocate a site specific to (each of three) particular (priestly) rites to smaller gatherings (known as guardians) within each Clan who were responsible for its maintenance and security. Knowledge of those distinct sites was even acknowledged externally between these and other Families or Clans prior to their dissociation (expressed here as 'for fear of persecution', though more) probably due to a decline in opportunity and interest in the post war aftermath of the 1950's.

Apparently, even though the Male and Female Mysteries had become combined decades before Bowers retrieved his legacy, it was his belief that this somehow denuded their distinctive virtue and it was his hope that the Male and Female Mysteries would once again be taught separately. He was also determined to confirm a working philosophy both compatible and in some ways comparable to the Kabbalah, yet presented on its own terms relative to Traditional Craft praxes. He refers again to these enigmatic formulae when discussing the Male and Female Mysteries to Joe Wilson, and to the 'order' of 1734. Within his many letters to ourselves, John pointed out more than once elements of traditions know to him prior to joining the Clan, happily shared in order to enflesh the bare bones known to Roy. One main input concerns the 'Rite of Seeing,' being one of the four 'arts' gifted to the each consecutive Magister of the Clan. The rite employed by Roy at that time was considered inadequate by John, who spoke disparagingly of it as: 'table rapping;' what he gave Roy changed the dynamic absolutely, having a resonance akin to nigromancy of true old craft practices.[cxxix]

Another note [cxxx] refers to the break-up of the Clan after Roy's death and how Chalky and George founded the Regency with material formulated jointly within the Clan, but developed according to their own vision, supplemented with other traditional material of their own, pre-clan. He describes how the guides essentially encourage and create change in order to keep the cauldron flowing. Roy had been aware of the concepts within the 'Rose Beyond the Grave, which needed the practical applications known to John. The Cave of the Cauldron was similarly enfleshed by George Winter:

"Roy had the basic mythos and concepts, but had not worked out the practicalities of putting them into practise. Those he encountered so late in life, could only offer him verbal knowledge, rather than take him through the actions in practise. He died young even before he'd fully worked all this out and put it together." [cxxxi]

Careful study of the works reveal the main differences as being Chalky and George's apparent preference for 'Celtic' myth and open paganism where Roy's and John's works were based staunchly in Anglo-Saxon lore. Holda, not Kerridwin, Odhin not Dagda, etc. In a very late letter John states:

"The snag with the Regency will always be – 'What are they working'? Chalky and George had their own system based on some of Roy's material and teachings, so if one wanted to be pedantic about it, they could claim to be kindred to Clan. Chalky and George never claimed Clan status for the Regency and neither do the new Regency people as far as I know." [cxxxii]

After the split, John had made his choice not to join Chalky and George, placing his preferential allegiance with Roy's widow when she asserted her decision to continue as the 'Clan.' [cxxxiii] Some years later, material turned up mysteriously on a certain historian's desk claiming to be from the Royal Windsor Coven. Once again however, close inspection revealed it as work belonging to the Regency that had found its self astray and put together and renamed for disingenuous purposes. Roy certainly added to this obfuscation, claiming in at least one letter, here to someone by the name of 'ickle deric' he had connections in Stafford and Windsor, which has led to considerable misunderstanding. [cxxxiv]

"In what passes as witchcraft today, there is as much illusion and unresolved desire as there is in the outside world. In the closed circles of some covens, there is greater bigotry and dogma than there is in many

sections of the moribund Christian church. Many witches appear to have turned their backs upon the reality of the outside world and have been content to follow, parrot fashion, the rituals and beliefs that they have little or no relationship with the 20th century and its needs"[cxxxv]

5. Wisdom: Evolution as the Spirit of Change

"The spirit of change is the ever present hungry wolf, prowling the periphery of stagnation."

This eventual shift from restrictive dogma, allows growth upon those foundations, fed by inspiration and personal intuition, honing praxis in accord with personal gnosis. The final teacher is the self. All keys passed through the sacred Covenant facilitate the evolution of the Clan in accord with the needs of its vital Egregore.

Bowers believed that wisdom comes only to those who earn it as the reward of spirit wherein the teacher is yourself 'seen through a mirror darkly.' Roy Bowers, atavistic spirit, former (late) Magister and founder of Clan Tubal Cain was convinced that but few genuine Cuveens were extant throughout the British Isles.

Thusly convinced he was the repository of almost three centuries of hereditary gnosis, he proselytised a surprisingly 'modern' perspective of Traditional Craft practices. His idiosyncratic expositions accentuated his innovative flair for evolutionary and militant interpretation. As a radical reformer of his religion he aspired to integrate disparate views, to consolidate them en masse in opposition to the then newly emerging and popular 'Wica' (sic).

Naturally, working methodologies differed considerably, in accord with their inherent philosophies, creeds, Mythos et cetera; yet some basic similarities prevailed, affording common ground, recognised and appreciated by all traditional practitioners of their arte. Even so he expounded his belief that instinctive and intuitive modus operandi were infinitely superior to dogmatic working by rote, asserting that form (Purusha - black, passive) that is, the structure and symbolism of the ritual was secondary to force (Prakriti - white, active) invoked, or how this virtue is won, maintained and assimilated. In this he recognised three basic ritual forms fundamental to those of the 'True Faith;' best exampled within 'The Three Rites' or 'Rings.'

In another letter, Bowers is keen to assert the three mysteries of the Clan somewhat wistfully with regard to the 'Tree of Life' depicted upon the

Monolith in Brittany: St. Uzec Menhir. These have been developed further still, extending his understanding relative to new insights and the Clan's rightful evolution. Both Maid and Magister embody the potencies of the Left and Right sides of the Tree upon the Menhir through the tools of Severity under the Moon and all the tools of Mercy under the Sun. [cxxxvi]

Symbols are a traditional device by which a quality is condensed and represented graphically. Naturally within the Clan of Tubal Cain we have our own understanding of what such symbols mean to us and how we would use them according to Clan Cosmology and its particular Mythos. Each one 'holds' an idea, waiting to inspire us. They contain something of the virtue of that which they represent. Context is everything. As such they can generate myriad comprehensions, so the intention of the artist hardly matters, as it is the viewer who 'reads' them. Layers of meaning need not conflict either. And these innovative correspondences do not in any way diminish those suggested by Roy Bowers, who like many true Masters be they Rabbis , Sheikhs, Priests, or Brahmins, were and are able to use whatever subject matter is to hand to express through analogous use of parable, a profound revelation.

During the seven years we knew and studied with Evan John Jones, former Magister of the Clan of Tubal Cain, many curious things, some of which seemed initially to have little use or relevance to what we were doing, have later revealed intensely profound expressions. He had cautioned us to be patient, to assimilate slowly the finer subtleties of the art, inexorably woven into the fabric of the Clan, hinting strongly, the seven year cycle relative to it. This osmotic process drew to it the newly inherited 'Egregore.' No one may teach, he insisted, until we have taught ourselves what the mysteries are. "Hopefully after the next cycle has transpired this may have evolved into wisdom. Through the work alone, does light dawn."[cxxxvii] The keys to understanding truth, Bowers has asserted more than once, lay with the guardians of each Tradition, discarnate ancestors and deific forms who benefit the next generation of spiritual heirs.

"Prayer is the ladder that binds the body to the earth whilst the soul ascends into the dizzying heights of the heavens."

Bowers understood the cyclic nature of wisdom asserting how its discovery "creates the alchemy that brings forth an answer." Among his many teachings the controversial and enigmatic '1734' numbers have generated abundant speculation. Often complex, they all reveal something of the poetic and individual nature of his work. Throughout the diverse ways this has been experienced and expressed within its own current of practitioners, to those of us within the Clan, the reality of its practise is deceptively simple: One 'Will' to open the seven gates to the triune (three) god of the four square garden. The solar cross of Clan Tubal Cain's compass essentially formulates the celestial substance of the central Monad, where four qualities cross-polarize in perfect balance. This central core or neutral zone is where one may achieve enlightenment - 'Unio Mystica'. Exogenous to the traditional nine knots of the witches ladder (four solar rites, four lunar rites, plus one other at Twelfth Night) are four additional rites that facilitate unfolding mystical pathways exemplified within Clan Tubal Cain as a seasonal quaternary. Alchemy is the science of God, our gift of transmutation from matter into spirit or the body of light and bliss - Premdeha.[cxxxviii]

"The Faith is finally concerned with Truth, total Truth. It is one of the oldest of religions, and also one of the most potent, bringing as it does, Man into contact with Gods, and Man into contact with Self." (Roy Bowers)

These words express the bounds of virtue, extended into a current, vital and vibrant clan, heirs to the rich tapestry of gnosis and Wyrd incumbent upon all vowed to its hearth. This research is dedicated to all those men, strong and true; to ladies fair and wise, to the work they lived for and the love they died for. And likewise, do we now in their wake. I thank you all, forever bound in troth to the nameless gods and faceless ancestors of our complex and diverse stream.

Chapter Sixteen

Elementary Praxes: Musings on the Aetts

Air: The Wind Gods.

O.E. windwian, from wind; *air in motion, paring down.* Cognate with O.N. vinza, O.H.G. winton *to fan,* winnow; Goth. diswinþjan *to throw* (grain) *apart* ;L. vannus *winnowing fan.*

Windyat: 'The Windyat' in this instance is clearly Odhin as Leader of the Wild Hunt.

There are several interpretations for this, two in particular reflect Roy Bowers' intent in this passage and they are both developed from old Germanic and gothic language roots- the first is a sense of pole [Qutub] as in the whip to the wind; the second implies a 'winnowing' of being threshed, thrown about, ground in the [wind] Mill itself.......

I have to say, it brings to mind the beautiful and evocative poem by Gibran in which he says:

"Like the sheaves of corn he gathers you unto himself.
He threshes you to make you naked.
He sifts you to free you from your husks.
He grinds you to whiteness.
He kneads you until you are pliant;
And then he assigns you to his sacred fire, that you may become sacred bread for God's sacred feast."

- North derives from the word for left. When facing the rising Sun, North falls naturally to your left. Significantly, it also means below. Many shamanic traditions maintain the Underworld, i.e. that which is below, as being North within the earth. In Northern traditions, the lower worlds of the World Tree, being colder were also deemed to be North, geographically. Therefore, to refer to any other direction as North, the original and vital meaning left is forfeit. *Needle/Spear & Thread/Norns [wind/air] {Dragon- Ond-Cosmic Breath}*

- South is believed to derive from *sunthaz* may the suggest Sun, but may also suggest its zenith; though nothing is proven. Importantly, Sunna, was feminine. *Hammer [earth/life] {Rock Giant- Od-magnetic forces}*

- East finds its origin in a word for the light of dawn. No other cardinal direction above the equator, and west of Arabia could use this in any other sense. *Distaff& Sword, [sun/heat/passion] {Bull-Orlog-Cosmic Me}*

- West signifies a *descent* as in the setting sun as it falls to the western seaboard, later described as the end of the day, or evening. No other direction makes sense for the word. *Necklace, [Seas/emotion/memory] {Eagle-Odhr-Inspiration}*

Roy's use of the cardinals perfectly reflects the ethos of the Northern Traditions. And so it is ideally placed within the British Isles and Northern Europe. Specifically, it makes sense of connections between direction, element and time of year/season.

North, Winter = wind, thus Air. As each person stands to face the North, the Mound and sacred origin of our ancestry, we have the rising sun, the glorious dawn, to the right/east; we have the setting sun, to our left/west and below we stand upon the earth and gaze upwards into the northern skies. It is humankind's most natural bi-polar, magnetic compass, self oriented.

Colours are also attributed to these directions, often considered *Celtic* in origin - this is in error.

Black is given to North. For the Void of the Winter Sky.

Red is given to the fiery, rising sun in the East. East is the Rising Sun. Fire and Red are very appropriate for the sun.

West presents the dying sun, falling into the deep waters at the close of each day, and become inexorably linked to the Land of the Dead, reached only by a great expanse of water. It is also the Well, the Cauldron and Marah. So the colour is Grey - shades of dusty twilight.

South/White: Britain's verdant earth, the land beneath our feet offers no finer position for Earth itself. It offers life and light, and is therefore White, like much of its native chalky and limey soils.

The Point and the Square.

The square is formed when the Jungian vitalities [mentioned in the alchemy of the compass] are attributed to the zodiac where they intersect the cardinal markers as follows: Spring, Summer, Autumn then Winter for completion.

This deosil/sunwise motion takes fire to water, to air ending with earth. This forms the 'square' portrayed in the three rites. It marks the themes of the solar rites and how each rite transmutes to the others in cumulative succession. Yule marks the grounding, quite literally of this cycle.

In contrast to this, despite apparent similarities, the cardinals denote the winds, whistled in to form the following pattern, which may be reversed depending upon purpose:

East to West and then North to South, crossing at the Centre, the vortex, or Compass Star, formed by the Point [of crossing].

Though both appear to follow the same 'elemental' pattern of fire, water, air and earth; they are vastly distinct.

The Square: follows the emotive qualities of the stellar and solar elements combined as they are drawn out from its predecessor [as water/Cancer is from fire/Aries at midsummer]. The Point follows the physical potencies of the elemental winds as they 'rush' in, binding themselves as the central vortex upon the 'point', the hearth, the ayin, the celestial 'Eye', thereto combine fire from all realms.

The first then, follows the [apparent] movement of sun, stars and moon. The second denotes the cross winds that howl unto the point, the central hearth and Axis Mundi.

One is expansive, fanning outwards, the other contracts inwards.

One is thus centripetal, the other centrifugal.

These correspondences clearly express the shifting nature of the elements, dependent upon how you perceive the element and through what it manifests.

In this, it can be shown how North = Air; but it also = Earth.

The Pale Leukathea is the multi-faceted jewel, of whom we see only one facet, the mirror of Venus beams down her subtle influences, her radiant magics of flux and stasis. Roy Bowers refers to *woman as the lesser moon*; this is because the tides of her body are in sync with that great silver orb in the heavens, and by which, in like fashion she generates, nurtures and controls creativity, intuition, emotion and all things of the *unconscious state.*

She is thus the presiding genius behind all creation, life and death. As Shakti, she is Mistress [and compliment] to the male mysteries.

She is all FORCE and by reflux is CHTHONIC.

She empowers His three Rites of the Mound, between All Hallows and Candlemas excluding Twelfth Night, which is the 9th rite of the year and is essentially the bridge itself that turns the mill form one cycle to the next.

LOVE.

This is symbolized on the Right Male Pillar by the upright triangle.

The man, the solitary wanderer and guardian is concerned with the ebb and flow of time, of logic and reason, of the elemental forces that forge the civilizing arts and sciences of the *conscious state*, thus he becomes Master [generating complement] to the female Mysteries.

He is all FORM and by reflux is TRANSCENDENCE.

He manifests Her five Rites between Spring Equinox to the Autumn Equinox.

TRUTH.

It is symbolized on the Left Female Pillar by the reversed pentagram.

Hence it can be seen how there are not 8 knots, but 5 and 3.

Together, time and fate become eternity/infinity - ∞

The Priestly Mysteries are concerned with lunar, solar and stellar rites, as found within the 3 Rings.

These are the Cave, the Castle and the Rose.

Three columns or pillars comprised of the two pillars of Tubal Cain [NE & NW] and the Central Qutub forming the V of the mound in the North (the < is also the symbol of Coma Berenice, seen in the skies above Virgo).

Together these formulate the five rings of the '*basic structure of the craft.*'

Chapter Seventeen

Transmission:

Three x Three x Three ~ Nine Realms, Worlds and Potencies

Three Magisters:

1. Roy Bowers ~ Lapwing {totem = boar}
2. Evan John Jones ~ Dog {totem = stag}
3. Terrence Oates ~ Roebuck {totem = ram}

Three Totems reflect the 'Tripartite Covenant'

"For many eons of time the human spirit had no abode, then finally by desire to survive created the pathway into the Otherworlds. Nothing is got by nothing and whatever we do now creates the world in which we exist tomorrow. The same applies to death, what we have created in thought we create in that other reality. We should also remember that Desire was the first of all created things.........When I am dead, I shall go to another place that myself and those who have gone before me have created. Without their work it would not exist; it was their Faith that built it and it is my believing in it that will secure my inheritance."

[Robert Cochrane 1966]

"So when we talk about the transmigrating soul, we visualise it as slowly progressing along an inwardly spiralling circle until it reaches the point of never having to return to this world again............I suppose one could say

that the real start of this journey comes when we first realise that the re-incarnating soul exists. Before this, the soul unknowingly progressed along the path up to the point when we as people realise this.........from this point on, an individual's spiritual destiny is in their own hands. What they choose to make of this destiny is up to them."

[Evan John Jones 1998]

"It is the purpose of Mystery Religions to re-organize the misaligned principals that impede spiritual growth. The goal of all true magic and religion is not ritual alone, for that is but a simple prop, a tool through which we direct our will towards contact - proof as opposed to mere Faith.

Those who live for myth and superstition alone are being deceived, and labouring under such restriction, will ultimately lose 'Faith,' unless cajoled or threatened. But the Underground Stream employs none of these methodologies. Everyone is encouraged to experience for themselves the face of the faceless one. Myths are just a way of explaining how the formless one can be understood. They cannot explain the agonies of the quest, nor the painful stripping away of the self, not even the rapture of revelation, which is not of death, but of life, here, now and beyond. This returns us to the point yet again of ignorance, of being distanced (exiled) from the Truth, the following repeated directive "EAT THIS BREAD IN THE DEVILS NAME WITH GIRT TERROR AND FEARFULL DREAD" stresses its real significance and one that is often overlooked."

[Robin-the-dart. 2003]

Virtue~Transmission~Maid to Magister to Maid

3 proofs of Virtue revealed though exemplary achievement by 3 separate trials to commence* after gesture of intent to pass the mantle:

1. Old Covenant/Law = Sacrifice*= Asgard {Priest of the Spirit}
2. Teaching = Submission* = Bifrost – the Bridge {Warrior of the Soul}
3. Title = Humility*= Midgardhr/Udgardhr/Hella {King /Sovereign of/over the Body}

First Trial: 3 pure states of being:

1. Mind - Thought ~ Master {of self}
2. Heart - Love ~ Journeyman
3. Speech - Truth ~ Apprentice

Second Trial: 3 psychopompic traps to beguile the ego:

1. Lapwing - Illusion ~ disguises the secret
2. Dog - Fear ~ guards the secret
3. Roebuck - Delusion ~ hides the secret

Third Trial: 3 gifts:

1. Of Spirit - Sight/foresight ~ that sees far beyond ~ Mercy
2. Of Soul - Compassion/grace ~ that in knowing, feels all ~ Empathy
3. Of Deed – Causality/honour ~ that abhors the lie ~ Justice

So, in actual practice, this complex list is expressed as follows:

Each of the three proofs of Virtue requires three trials, each of three parts, awarding one for each of three realms, of all three worlds, giving nine qualities in total.

As the Apprentice, the prospective candidate [named by intent – i.e. TITLE] must begin the Midgardhr level of each of the three trials.

These entail: a state of being, a challenge to the ego and a gift.

Thus, through Truth as the starting point and <u>First Trial</u>, the Apprentice comes to live within Maat. No progression can be made without first acting in, and understanding the Truth as a <u>State of Being</u>.

The <u>Second Trial</u>, presents the challenge to the ego, where the Apprentice as the 'Roebuck' needs to understand the principle of the Secret, what it is and how to preserve it by keeping it hidden. The Ego will attempt to assume 'superiority' believing it withholds a great treasure from the many for the few, inducing a sense of elitism. This <u>State of Delusion</u> must be overcome.

<u>The Third Trial</u>, requires the Apprentice to understand the principle of Causality within the material world, how then to act with Honour, maintaining Truth whilst avoiding the ego-trap of delusion, in order to correctly administer <u>Justice</u>, where this is deemed appropriate. This <u>Deed</u> is one undertaken in the 'rightness of things', to recognise the Lie and act appropriately.... justice is never vengeance, nor is it retaliation. It is the merit of all causality – True Karma.

Completion of these three trials on the level of Midgardhr, brings Humility*, which is the 3rd proof of Virtue.

Next, the level of Bifrost, being the Bridge, fords Midgardhr with Asgardhr and is cognate in many ways with the Middle Pillar. Here the candidate, having accomplished the three trials as an Apprentice, must now repeat them as Journeyman.

First Trial: the work undertaken through love, via the path of the heart unconquerable passion and conviction in one's Faith to the Journeyman. This State of Being, generates the purity of love as a powerful source of strength to one's self and others; it allows the flow of constructive evolution through understanding, free of bias and judgmentalisms.

Second Trial: the awareness of the ego-trap through the responsibility of guardianship of the secret. The Dog, is ferocious, but not fearless. The Journeyman must learn to respect, understand and transmute fear in themselves and others in order to strengthen their ability to be an effective guardian.

Third Trial: The Gift here, being of the heart, is Compassion, the ability to receive and confer grace – it is acquired through true empathy.

Completion of these three trials on the level of Bifrost, brings Submission,* being the potency of [ego-less]Teaching, which is the 2nd proof of Virtue.

Finally, of being, Self-Mastery is acquired on the level of Asgardhr completed through the First of the three final trials, [of being, of challenge and the gift]. The Mind, must acquire the skill of distinction and discernment, free of ego, judgment, yet expressing compassion, with honour, through truth.

Second Trial: The Lapwing alerts us to the folly of illusion, of distractions of the Mind that cause us to miss what we know is unreal, for what we perceive through artifice and disingenuity. The Secret may only be observed and apprehended if we witness if free of visual sleight of hand.

Final Trial: Offering foresight, Spirit perhaps offers us the most fragile of gifts; yet through the visions it facilitates, Mercy may be offered keenly or withheld, where knowledge is an imperative factor, a central key to action. Error is humankind's greatest vitality; forgiveness awarded through Mercy is a divine gift. It is to be cherished and dispensed with true awareness.

And so Completion of these final trials awards the Mastery of Self, through Sacrifice, to Self and to the Cause, to the Law, in fact. Such is the Old Covenant, the final act undertaken between the newly appointed Master and their predecessor in the Glorious and beautiful ~

'Sun and Moon Rite.'

Thus do the 3 become 9, become 1, or the hunter, the hunted and Old Tubal!

The Old Covenant Stang conjures the images of the *Huluppa Tree* of Bird, Goddess and Tree, covering the Three Realms of the Sacred Mé.

Irmin's blazing chariot spinning around the heavens is the haywain – the cart of Nerthus.

These are the sacred laws of descent and ascent = The Faith. Three parts, three mysteries, three gods, three elements all spinning around a primal centre. The central column of Irminsul, upholds the heavens, literally separating them from collapse upon the earth. It is the scales of balance, weighing order and chaos, war with mercy for truth and justice. Within the Compass it is predominant across it, above it and around it. It is Gungnir, the spear of destiny, hence the Fates.

The core principle of the Faith is the Covenant, particularly in the sense of *'religio'* that is , to bind back, to bind all of us back to the primal understanding of our three-fold nature reflected by the three-fold deity. We are composed of body, spirit and soul. All three are bound in Faith to that principle; through these three aspects the Old Covenant 'en-titles.'

All four cardinal totems exhibit these triple aspects through their poles, having points fore, left and right…be these wings, labrys, or horns. Four totems, each of three points, each three become One.

Thus the Covenant is refracted throughout the Compass. Together, they form the Holy Sacred, 'Wind Rose of Anu.' Anu, the atom, the point of time, the God of the Sun, who rules the winds.

The Bright Home of Valhalla, Odhin's Hall is located in Gladsheimr. Twelve seats are said to wait for the twelve true warriors to return. Is it too much to suppose they could be arranged in a circle? Within Teutonic Myth, the Wisdom Goddess sits upon a throne within crystal enclosure beneath flowing waters. Known as Saga meaning wisdom, she was much consulted and highly revered.

The Creation Epic states how the world was created from slaying the giant Ymir, and how the first of humankind was created from two trees – the Ash and the Alder [*ask & embla*].

All the children of Ymir were said to have drowned in the flood created by his blood when he was killed, that is, all except one - Bergelmir, who survives in a boat and fathers more giants.

Odhin gave the gift of Life to the fledgling soul of humankind. Honir gave intellect; Lodur gave them blood and colour.

The Walkyries/disir choose their OWN dead, that is their own filial descendants, Clan and tribal specific to each of the *24 wind spirits or flygia,* who carry home the souls of those known to them as kin.

WITHIN the unchanging twilight
Of the high land of the gods,
Between the murmuring fountain
And the Ash-tree, tree of trees,
The Norns, the terrible maidens,
For evermore come and go.

Yggdrasill the populous Ash-tree,
Whose leaves embroider heaven,
Fills all the gray air with music—
To Gods and to men sweet sounds,
But speech to the fine-ear'd maidens
Who evermore come and go.

That way to their doom stead thrones
The Aesir ride each day,
And every one bends to the saddle
As they pass beneath the shade;
Even Odin, the strong All-father,
Bends to the beautiful maidens
Who cease not to come and go.

The tempest crosses the high boughs,
The great snakes heave below,
The wolf, the boar, and antler'd harts
Delve at the life-giving roots,

But all of them fear the wise maidens,
The wise-hearted water-bearers
Who evermore come and go.

And men far away, in the night-hours
To the north-wind listening, hear;
They hear the howl of the were-wolf,
And know he hath felt the sting
Of the eyes of the potent maidens
Who sleeplessly come and go.
They hear on the wings of the north-wind
A sound as of three that sing;
And the skald, in the blae mist wandering
High on the midland fell,
Heard the very words of the o'ersong
Of the Norns who come and go.

But alas for the ears of mortals
Chance-hearing that fate-laden song!
The bones of the skald lie there still:
For the speech of the leaves of the Tree
Is the song of the three Queens [cxxxix]
Maidens who evermore come and go.

[William Bell Scott(1811–90]

APPENDICES

Appendix One

Odhin & Tyr Table

Odhin	*Tyr*
Bi-polar [as in 'change'] Aesir = male/ north and east/air and fire	Uni-polar [that is of singular focus] Vanir = female/ South and west/earth and water
Wanderer Warrior – conquest and victory	Stability – fixed- nowl star-bright glory Warrior – truth, honour, justice.
Deception/deceit/trickery	Honour/truth/oaths
Valfather – chooser of the slain	Binder of chaos
Master of wild beasts: wolf, raven, Horse, eagle and worm/dragon	Tamer of the beast
Fertility and harvest	Associations with the 'thing'
Patron of skalds, poetry and mead	Binder of oaths Sacrifice & humility Religious instinct within man
Freyja taught him knowledge of runes, Seidr and galdr	Separates heaven and earth via its imposing central column – axis mundi Anima mundi/world soul

Appendix Two

Valkyrie Names

[cxl] Valkyrie names

1. Alruna (ON Ölrún, Old german Ailrun) is a Germanic female personal name, from Proto-Germanic 'secret, rune' + 'noble' ON 'ale rune') Valkyrie. It is also the name for the *mandragora* or mandrake plant:
2. Brynhildr (Brünnhilde, Brynhild) is a Shield maiden and Valkyrie.
3. Eir (ON 'help, mercy') a goddess and/or Valkyrie associated with medical skill.. In addition, Eir has been theorized as a form of the goddess Frigg and has been compared to the Greek goddess Hygeia.
4. Geiravör (ON 'spear -vör') is a Valkyrie
5. Vor – 'spear goddess'
6. Göndul (ON 'wand –wielder') is a Valkyrie.
7. Gunnar or Gunner is a Valkyrie in Norse Myth. Her name means 'battle' and is cognate with the English word 'gun'. She rode a wolf assisted in the selection of the dead warriors together with two other Valkyries in order to bring them to Valhalla.
8. Herfjötur (ON 'host-fetter' or 'fetter of the army') is a Valkyrie. Kenning that probably refers to the 'fortune determining function of the Valkyries especially in battle.'
9. Herja (ON) is a Valkyrie - meaning "devastate 'goddess of war'."
10. Hlaðguðr svanhvít (Old Norse "Hlaðguðrswan -white" is a Valkyrie.
11. Hildr (ON 'battle') is a Valkyrie, power to revive the dead in battlefields & battle
12. Hervör alvitr (Old Norse, alvitr possibly meaning 'all-wise' or 'strange creature' a Valkyrie. the seven-year wife of the smith Volundr.
13. Hlökk (ON 'noise, battle') is a Valkyrie.

14. Kára is a Valkyrie. 'The wild, stormy one' (based on Old Norse afkárr, meaning 'wild') or "curl" or 'the curly one' (from Old Norse kárr 'the one with the (long?) Odin's curls.'

15. Mist (ON 'Cloud' or 'mist') is a Valkyrie. Literal meaning - Valkyries ride through the air and over water.

16. Róta is a Valkyrie mentioned alongside the Valkyries Gunnr and Skuldee, and the three are described as "always [riding] to choose who shall be slain and to govern the killings."

17. Sigrdrífumál 'sayings of the victory-bringer', also known as Brynhildarljóð

18. Sigrún (ON 'victory rune') is a Valkyrie

19. *Skögul (ON 'shaker' or possibly 'high-towering') and Geirskögul (Old Norse 'spear-skögul') are Valkyrie who alternately appear as separate or individual figures

20. Skulde (the name possibly means debt or future) is also a Norn in Norse Myth. Along with Urdhr (ON 'fate' and Verdandi (possibly 'happening' or 'present', Skulde makes up a trio of Norns that are described as *deciding the fates* of people, Skulde appears in at least two poems as a Valkyrie.

21. Svipul (ON 'changeable') is a Valkyrie synonym for 'battle' - changeable nature of fate,

22. Þrúðhr (ON 'strength'), anglicized as Thrúd or Thrud, Serves ale in Valhalla

23. Völuspá (Old Norse V▯luspá, Prophecy of the Volva (Seeress)

24. Grímnismál (Sayings of Grímnir). It is spoken through the voice of Grímnir, one of the many guises of the god Odhin.

Appendix Three

Etymology of Goda

368 गोद goda. गोविद् go-vid.

गोद 2. goda, m. n. the brain, L.

गोदान 2. godāna, n. (dāna, fr. √do? 'place where the hair (go) is cut,' Ragh. iii, 33, Sch.) the side-hair, ŚBr. iii; KātyŚr.; PārGṛ.; = -maṅgala, ĀśvGṛ.; Kauś.; ŚāṅkhGṛ.; Gobh.; Gaut.; R. —maṅgala, n. a ceremony performed with the side-hair of a youth of 16 or 18 years (when he has attained puberty and shortly before marriage), R. (G) i, 73, 22. —vidhi, m. id., Ragh. iii, 33.

Godānika, mfn. = gaud°, Gobh. iii, 1, 28.

गोदानीय godānīya, &c. See gó, p. 365, col. 1.

Go-dāvarī, go-duh, &c. See ib.

गोध godha, m. pl., N. of a people, MBh. vi, 9, 42 (rodha, C).

गोधन go-dhana, -dhara, &c. See gó, p. 365.

गोधा godhā, f. (g. bhidādi) a sinew (cf. gó), RV. x, 28, 10 & 11; AV. iv, 3, 6; a chord, RV. viii, 69, 9; a leathern fence wound round the left arm to prevent injury from a bow-string, MBh. iii, iv, vii; R. i, ii; an Iguana (either the Gosamp or the alligator, commonly gosāpa), VS. xxiv, 35; Bṛih.; Mn. &c.; = -vatī, Gal.; N. of the authoress of a Sāman. —padikā, f. Cissus pedata, L. —padī, f. (g. kumbhapady-ādi) id., L. —vatī, f. the plant Irāvatī, L. —vīṇākā, f. a kind of stringed instrument, KātyŚr. xiii, 3, 17. —°śana (°dhāś°), m. 'Iguana-eater,' N. of a man, v.l. for go-vāsana. —sāman, n. the Sāman of Godhā, ĀrshBr. —skandha, m. Vachellia farnesiana (viṭ-khadira), L.

Godhāya, Nom. P. °yati, to move curvedly like an Iguana, g. kaṇḍv-ādi (Gaṇar. 439).

Godhāra, m. = gaudh°, Kād. v, 1042 (v.l.)

2. Godhi, m. id., L.

Godhikā, f. a kind of lizard or alligator (Lacerta Godica), Kād. v, 1042 (v. l. golikā). Godhikātmaja, m. a kind of lizard, L.

Godhinī, f. a variety of Solanum, L.

Godheraka, m. = gaudh°, Suśr. v, 8, 36.

गोधूम go-dhūma, &c. See gó, p. 365, col. 1.

गोधेर godhera, m. (= guh°) a guardian, L.

गोधेरक godheraka. See godhā.

गोनन्द go-nanda, -narda, &c. See gó, p. 365.

गोप go-pá, m. (= -pā s.v. gó) a cowherd, herdsman, milkman (considered as a man of mixed caste, Parāś.), Mn. viii; MBh. (ifc. f. ā, i, 3213); Hariv. &c.; a protector, guardian, RV. x, 61, 10; TāṇḍyaBr.; KātyŚr.; MBh.; the superintendent of several villages, head of a district, L.; a king, L.; 'chief herdsman,' Kṛishṇa, MBh. ii, 1438; a particular class of plants, BhP. xii, 8, 21; = -rasa, L.; N. of a Gandharva (cf. go-pati), R. ii, 91, 44; of a Buddh. Arhat, W.; (ā), f., N. of one of the wives of Śākya-muni, Lalit. xii &c.; cf. gaupeya; Ichnocarpus frutescens, L.; (ī), f. id., L.; (Vop. iv, 22; cf. Pāṇ. iv, 1, 48) a cowherd's wife, Hit. ii, 7, 1/2; a cowherdess, milkmaid (esp. the cowherdesses of Vṛindāvana, companions of Kṛishṇa's juvenile sports, considered sometimes as holy or celestial personages; cf. RTL. pp. 113 & 136), MBh. ii, 2291; Hariv. 4098; BhP.; Gīt.; a protectress, female guardian, Ragh. iv, 20 (ifc.); = prakṛiti, nature, Kramadīp.; Abrus precatorius, L.; (cf. ahi-, indra-, kula-, tri-daśa-, vāta-, surêndra-.) —kanyakā, f. a cowherdess, Hariv. 4095. —kanyā, f. id., 4081 & 4085; the gopā plant, Bhpr. v. —karkaṭikā, f. = gopāla-karkaṭī, L. —ghaṇṭa, m. Flacourtia sapida, Gal. —ghaṇḍā, f. id., Suśr. v, 7, 1. —ghoṇṭā, f. id., i, iv. —jalā, f. = go-capalā, VāyuP. ii, 37, 122. —jīvin, m., N. of a mixed caste. —tā, f. a herdsman's office, Hariv. 3302. —tva, n. id., 3160 ff. —daṭṭa, m., N. of a Buddh. author. —danta, m., N. of an author, Uṇ. iv, 16, Sch. —dala, m. the betel-nut tree, L. —nagara, n., N. of a town. —bhaṭṭa, v.l. for go-bh°. —bhadra, n. the fibrous esculent root of a water-lily, L.; (ā), f. = -bhadrikā, L. —bhadrikā, f. Gmelina arborea, L. —rasa, m. myrrh, L. —rāshṭra, m. pl., N. of a people, MBh. vi, 351. —vadhū, f. a cowherd's wife, BhP. i, 9, 40; the gopī plant, Bhpr. —vadhūṭī, f. the youthful wife of a cowherd, Bhāshāp. 1. —vallī, f. the gopā plant, Suśr. vi, 51, 24; Sanseviera Roxburghiana, L. —vesha, mfn. dressed as a herdsman, Megh. Gopâgrahāra, m. pl., N. of several Agrahāras, Rājat. i, 343. Gopâcala, m. 'cowherd-mountain,' = gopāla-giri, Uttamac.³ 602. Gopâditya, m., N. of a king of Kaśmīr, Rājat. i, 341; N. of a poet. Gopâdri, m. = °pâcala, 343. Gopâdhyaksha, m. an overseer of herdsmen, chief herdsman, MBh. iv, 1155. Gopânasī, f. the wood or bamboo frame-work of a thatch, Lalit. xiv, 34; xvii; Kāraṇḍ.; Car. i, 30, 3; Śiś. iii, 49. Gopā-putra, see go-pá, s.v. gó. Gopâshṭamī, f. the 8th day in the light half of month Kārttika (on which Kṛishṇa who had formerly been a keeper of calves became a cowherd; cows are esp. to be worshipped on this day), KūrmaP. Gopêndra, m. 'chief herdsman,' Kṛishṇa, MBh. vi, 799; N. of the author of Kāvyālaṃkāra-dhenu. Gopêśa, m. (= °pêndra) Kṛishṇa, W.; N. of Nanda (Kṛishṇa's foster-father), Vop. v, 7; of Śākya-muni, L. Gopêśvara, m. a form of Śiva; N. of a man; -tîrtha, n., N. of a Tīrtha, RevāKh. ccxliv, ccl.

Gopaka, m. (g. yājakâdi, Gaṇar. 99, Sch.) a cowherd, Dhūrtan.; (fr. gopaya) guardian (ifc.), see cīvara-; the superintendent of a district, L.; myrrh, L.; (ikā), f. (g. kṣiprâdi) a cowherd's wife, cowherdess, BhP. x, 9, 14 f.; a protectress, W.

Gopat, mfn. = °payat, Gīt. vi, 12.

Gópana, n. (√gup) guarding, protection, preservation, AV. xii, 4, 10; MBh. vi, xiii; hiding, concealment, Sāh.; Sarvad.; Kull. on Mn. ix, 72; reviling, abuse, W.; flurry, hurry, alarm, W.; light, lustre, W.; the leaf of Laurus Cassia, L.; (ā), f. protection, ŚBr. iii, 6, 2, 12 & 15; MBh. xii, 11907.

Gopanīya, mfn. to be preserved or protected, Nāḍipr.; to be prevented, MBh. xii, 5399; to be concealed or hidden (with abl.), Sāh. vi, [illegible]; secret, mysterious, W. —tā, f. concealableness, W. —tva, n. id., W.

Gopaya, caus. fr. √gup or Nom. P. Ā. (fr. go-pá; cf. √gup) °yati, °yate (aor. Ved. 2. du. ajūgupatam, Pāṇ. iii, 1, 50, Kāś.), to guard, protect, preserve, ŚāṅkhŚr.; MBh. (Pass. gopyate, ii, iii); BhP.; to keep, VarBṛS. lxxxix, 13; to hide, conceal, keep secret, Pañcat.; RV. i, 11, 5, Sāy.; Mn. x, 59, Kull.; 'to speak' or 'to shine,' Dhātup. xxxiii, 98; (cf. abhi-, pra-, sam-.)

Gopayátya, mfn. (Nir. v, 1) to be protected, RV. viii, 25, 13.

Gopayitavya, mfn. v.l. for °pāy°.

1. Gopāya, Nom. P. (fr. go-pá; cf. √gup) °yáti (cf. Pāṇ. iii, 1, 28 & 31; aor. agopāyīt, Vop. viii, 65), to represent a cowherd, act like a herdsman, BhP. x, 30, 17; to guard, protect, preserve, RV. vi, 74, 4 & x, 154, 4; VS.; AV. &c.; to hide, conceal, Amar. (Pass. gopāyyate); Rājat. v, 222; Dhūrtas. i, 30: Caus. gopāyayati, to preserve, protect, MBh. iii, 10835; (cf. abhi-, pari-.)

2. Gopāya, mfn. ifc. preserving, Āp. i, 4, 24.

Gopāyaka, mfn. id., W.

Gopāyana, mfn. id., MBh. vi, 3131; m. N. of a teacher, VāmP. vi (v.l. go-māyu), cf. Smṛitik. ii, 4, 3; n. protecting, preserving, protection, ŚāṅkhGṛ. iii, 10, 2; Hariv. 2142; R. vii, 4, 9.

Gopāyita, mfn. preserved, protected, L.

Gopāyitavya, mfn. to be hidden, Kād. vi, 400.

Gopāyitṛi, m. a protector, MBh. xii, 8726.

Gopika, m. the Mokshaka tree, Gal.

Gopikā, f. of °paka, q.v. —saras, n., N. of a lake, SkandaP.

Gopita, mfn. preserved, guarded, MBh. i, iii; guarded (as the senses), kept in subjection, Divyâv.; concealed, kept secret, Kathās. xiv; Rājat. v, 124.

Gopinī, f. the gopā plant, L.

Gopila, mfn. (g. sakhy-ādi, v.l.) one who preserves or protects, L.

Gópishṭha, mfn. superl. of goptṛi, q.v.

Gopī, f. of °pa, q.v. —candana, n. a species of white clay (said to be brought from Dvārakā and used by Vishṇu's worshippers for marking the face, RTL. pp. 67 & 400; 'a kind of sandal-wood,' W.); °nôpanishad, f., N. of an Up. —nātha, m. 'lord of the cowherdesses,' Kṛishṇa; N. of several men; -sapta-śatī, f., N. of a work (perhaps = govardhana-ś°). —premâmṛita, n. 'nectar of (Kṛishṇa's) love for the cowherdesses,' N. of a work. —ramaṇa, m. 'lover of cowherdesses,' N. of a man, Kshitīś. v, 3 ff. —rasa-vivaraṇa, n., N. of a work.

Goptavya, mfn. to be preserved, MBh. xii, 3449.

Goptṛi, mf(trī, ŚBr.; Gobh.; MBh. xiii)n. (g. yājakâdi, Gaṇar. 99) one who preserves or protects or defends or cherishes, AV.; TS. vi; TBr.; ŚBr. (superl. gópishṭha, ii); ĀśvGṛ. &c. (n. °ptṛi, BhP. vii, 10, 28); one who conceals anything (in comp.), Yājñ. i, 310. —mat, mfn. having a protector, Kaush-Up. ii, 1.

Gopya, mfn. (Pāṇ. iii, 1, 114, Kāś.) to be preserved or protected, MBh. xii, 1481; to be kept or taken care of (a pledge, ādhi), Yājñ. ii, 59; to be kept secret or hidden, Daś. viii, 80 (superl.); Pañcat.; Kathās.; Hit.; m. a servant, slave, L.; the son of a female slave, L.

Gopyaka, m. a slave, servant, L.

गोपालव gopālava, m. pl., N. of a family of Brāhmans, Pāṇ. v, 3, 114, Kāś.

गोफिल gophila, g. sakhy-ādi (gobh°, Bhoj.; gop° & goh°, vv. ll.)

Gobhila, m., N. of the author of Pushpas. and of the Gṛihya-sūtra of the SV. (said to have also composed a Śrauta-sūtra and a Naigeya-sūtra); pl. N. of a family, Pravar. v, 4 (v.l. go-bida).

Gobhilīya, mfn. relating to or proceeding from Gobhila.

गोरट goraṭa, m. a kind of Acacia, L.

गोरण goraṇa = gur°, L., Sch.

गोरटिका goriṭikā, f. = go-rāṭikā, L.

गोर्द gorda, n. = goda, W.

Gordha, n. id., L.

गोर्वर gor-vara. See gó, p. 367, col. 3.

गोल gola, m. (= guḍa) 'a ball,' see -krīḍā; globe (as the celestial globe or as the globe of the sun or of the earth), Sūryas.; Sūryapr.; BhP. &c.; a hemisphere (of the earth), Sūryas.; = -yantra, Gol. xi, 2; Vangueria spinosa, L.; myrrh, L.; a widow's bastard, Yājñ. i, 222; VarP.; Śūdradh.; the conjunction of all the planets in one sign, Laghuj. x, 11; N. of a country, Romakas. (cf. golla); of a son of Ākrīḍa, Hariv. (kola, ed. Calc.); n. & (ā), f. a circle, sphere (maṇḍala), L.; a large globular water-jar, L.; (ā), f. a ball to play with, L.; red arsenic, L.; ink, L.; a woman's female friend, L.; N. of Durgā, L.; of a river (= go-dā or go-dāvarī), L.; (cf. gala-golin.) —krīḍā, f. playing with balls, Hariv. 15542 ff. —gola, m. a globe consisting of several globes, Sūryapr. —grāma, m., N. of a village (situated on the Godāvarī). —puñja, m. a number of globes, Sūryapr. —yantra, n. a kind of astronomical instrument, Gol. xi, 3. Golâṅka, m., N. of a man, g. aśvâdi (°ṅkya, Kāś.) Golâdhyāya, m. N. of ch. i of Bhāskara's Siddhânta-śiromaṇi treating of the terrestrial and celestial globes. Golâvalī, f. a series of globes, Sūryapr. Golâsana, n. 'ball-thrower,' a kind of gun, Gal.

Golaka, m. a ball or globe, BhP. v, 16, 4; VS. xxxi, 22, Sch. &c.; a ball for playing with, Hariv. 15549; glans penis, Sāy. on AitBr. i, 20; a kind of pease (= palāśa), Gobh. iv, 4, 26; ŚāṅkhGṛ. iv, 19, 4; myrrh, L.; a globular water-jar, L.; a kind of dish, Gal.; a widow's bastard, Mn. iii, 156 & 174; MBh. iii, 13366; the conjunction of all the planets in one sign, VarBṛ. xii, 3 & 19; N. of a pupil of Deva-mitra, VāyuP. i, 60, 64; n. a ball or globe, Nyāyam., Sch.; = go-loka, Tantr.; (ikā), f. a small ball or globule, SāmavBr. iii, 4, 3; (used for playing) HPariś.; the jujube, Gal.; for godhikā, q.v.

Goli-gula-parivartana, for go-lāṅg°, Lalit. iii, 88 f.

गोलत्तिका go-láttikā, &c. See gó, p. 366, col. 3.

Go-lava, °vaṇa, -lāṅgula, &c. See ib.

गोलाममामुद golāma-māmuda, غلام محمود.

गोलास golāsa, m. a fungus, L.

गोलिह go-liha, -līḍha. See gó, p. 366.

गोलुन्द golunda, N. of a man, g. gargâdi.

गोलोक go-loka, -loman, &c. See gó, p. 366.

गोल्ल golla, N. of a country, Hariś. viii, 194; (cf. gola.)

गोल्हाट golhāṭa, a kind of mystical diagram, Rasik. xiv, 34.

गोवत्स go-vatsa, &c. See gó, p. 366, col. 3.

गोवय govaya, Nom. P. (for gopaya) °yati, to keep off from (abl.), TāṇḍyaBr. xvi, 2, 3 f.

गोवर go-vara, °rdhana, &c. See gó, p. 366.

Go-vid, go-vinda, &c. See ib.

[cxli]Note variants:

[1] *Goda*: m. The 'Brain';

[2] *Godha*: m. pl. name of a 'people';

[3] *Godha*: f. chord/binding to left arm [past which signifies ancestry];

[4] *Godhera*: m. guardian

Conclusion: Egregore!

Appendix Four

List of Odhin's Names

Aldaföðr	Father of Men
Aldagautr	Gautr of Men
Aldingautr	The Ancient Gautr
Alfaðir, Alföðr	All-Father
Angan Friggjar	Delight of Frigg
Arnhöfði	Eagle-headed One
Atriði, Atriðr	Attacking Rider or Attacker by Horse
Auðun	Wealth Friend
Bági ulfs	Enemy of the Wolf
Baldrsfaðir	Father of Balder
Báleygr	Feeble Eye or Flame Eyed
Biflindi	Shield Shaker or Spear Shaker
Bileygr	Feeble Eye or One Eyed
Björn	Bear
Blindi, Blindr	Blind One
Bölverkr	Bale-worker
Böðgæðir	Battle Enhancer
Bragi	Chieftain
Bróðir Vilis / Vilja	Brother of Vili
Bruni, Brunn	Brown One
Burr Bors	Son of Borr
Darraðr, Dorruðr	Spearman
Draugadróttin	Lord of Ghosts
Ein sköpuðr galdra	Sole Creator of Magical Songs
Ennibrattr	One with a Straight Forehead
Eyluðr	Island Vessel? or Ever-Booming
Faðmbyggvir Friggjar	Dweller in Frigg's Embrace
Frumverr Friggjar	First Husband of Frigg
Faðir galdrs	Father of Magical Songs
Farmaguð, Farmatýr	Cargo God
Farmoguðr	Journey-Empowerer
Farmr arma Gunnlaðar	Burden of Gunnlöð's Arms
Farmr galga	Gallows' Burden
Fengr	Snatch or Gain
Fimbultýr	Mighty God
Fimbulþulr	Mighty Thule (Poet)
Fjölnir	Very-Wise or Concealer

Fjölsviðr, Fjölsvinnr	Much Wise
Foldardróttinn	Lord of the Earth
Frariðr	One Who Rides Forth
Frumverr Friggjar	First husband of Frigg
Fundinn	The Found
Gagnráðr	Contrary Advisor or Gainful Council
Galdraföðr	Father of Galdor (Magical Songs)
Gallow's Lord	
Gangleri	Wanderer, Waywont or Wayweary
Gangráðr	Journey Advisor
Gapthrosnir	One in a Gaping Frenzy
Gauti, Gautr	One from Gotland
Gausus	Gautr (Latinized Langobardic version) 1
Geiguðr	Dangler
Geirloðnir	Spear Inviter
Geirtýr	Spear God
Geirvaldr	Spear Master
Geirölnir	Spear Charger
Geldnir	?
Gestr	Guest
Gestumblindi	The Blind Guest
Ginnarr	Deceiver
Gizurr	Riddler
Gizurr Grýtingaliði	Gizurr, Companion of the Greutungi
Glapsviðr	Seducer
Goði hrafnblóts	Goði (priest) of the Raven-offering (worship)
Godjaðarr	God Protector
Gods' Atoner, The	
Gollnir, Gollor, Gollungr	Yeller
Göndlir	Wand Bearer
Gramr Hliðskjalfar	King of Hliðskjalf
Grímnir, Grímr	The Masked One or The Hooded One
Grímr	Masked, Grim
Gunnlod's Embracer	
Gunnar	Warrior
Gunnblindi	Battle Blinder
Guodan	Master of Fury (Romanised Langobardic)
Guodan, Gudan	Master of Fury (Westphalian)
Hagvirkr	Skillful Worker
Hangaguð	Hanged God
Hangagoð	God of the Hanged
Hangi	Hanged One

Haptabeiðir	Ruler of Gods
Haptaguð	God of Gods, God of Men or God of Prisoners
Haptasnytrir	Teacher of gods
Haptsönir	Fetter Loosener
Hár	High One
Hárbarðr	Hoar Beard or Grey Beard
Hárr	One Eyed
Harri Hliðskjalfar	Lord of Hliðskjalf
Hávi	High One
Heimþinguðr hanga	Visitor of the Hanged
Helblindi	Blinder With Death or Host Blinder
Helmet-capped Educator	
Hengikjopt	Hang Jaw
Herföðr, Herjaföðr	Host Father
Hergautr	Host Gautr
Herjan, Herran	Lord, Raider, or The One of the Host
Herteitr	Host Glad or Glad of War or Glad in Battle
Hertyr	Host God
Hildolfr	Battle Wolf
Hjaldrgoð	God of battle
Hjaldrgegnir	Engager of Battle
Hjálmberi	Helm Bearer
Hjarrandi	Screamer
Hlefreyr	Famous Lord or Mound Lord
Hild's Noise Maker (hild = battle)	
Hnikarr, Hnikuð	Inciter, Thruster or Shaker
Hoarr	One Eyed
Hotter	Hatter
Hovi	High One
Hrafnfreistuðr	Raven-tester
Hrafnáss	Raven God
Hrammi	Fetterer or Ripper
Hrani	Blusterer
Hrjotr	Roarer
Hroptatýr	Lord of Gods, God of Gods or Tumult God
Hroptr	God or The Maligned One or The Hidden One
Hrossharsgrani	Horse-hair Mustache
Hvatmoðr	Whet Courage (Mood)
Hveðrungr	Roarer
Itreker	Splendid Ruler
Jafnhár	Just As High

Jalfaðr	Yellow-brown Back
Jálg, Jálkr	Gelding
Jarngrimr	Iron Grim
Jolfr	Horse-wolf or Bear
Jölföðr	Yule-father
Jölnir	Yule
Jormundr	Mighty One
Karl	Old Man
Kjalarr	Nourisher or Keel Ruler
Langbarðr	Long Beard
Loðungr	Shaggy Cloak Wearer
Lord of Light	
Lord of the Wild Hunt , Wilde Jaeger	
Niðr Bors	Son of Borr
Njotr	User or Enjoyer
Óðinn	Frenzied One (Old Norse)
Óðr	Frenzy, Divine Inspiration, Breath
Odroerir's Gainer	
Ofnir	Opener, Entangler, Weaver or Inciter
Olgir	Protector? or Hawk
Ómi	Boomer or One Whose Voice Resounds
Óski	Wished For or Fulfiller of Desire
Ouvin	Master of Fury (Faroese)
Rauðgrani	Red Moustache
Reiðartyr	Wagon God
Rognir	Chief
Runatyr	God of Runes
Runni vagna	Mover of Constellations
Sanngetall	Truth Getter or He Who Guesses Right
Sannr, Saðr, Sath	Truth, The Truthful
Siðgrani	Longbeard
Siðhottr	Slouch Hat or Broad Brim or Deep Hood
Siðskeggr	Long Beard, or Broad Beard
Sigðir	Victory Bringer
Sigföðr	Father of Victory
Siggautr	Victory Gautr
Sigmundr	Victory Protection
Sigrhofundr	Victory Author
Sigrúnnr	Victory Tree
Sigthror	Victory Successful
Sigtryggr	Victory Sure

Sigtýr	Victory God
Skilving, Skilfing	King, or Trembler
Skollvaldr	Treachery Ruler
Sonr Bestlu	Son of Bestla
Spjalli Gauta	Friend of the Goths
Speedy One, The	
Sváfnir	Luller to Sleep (or Dreams), or Closer
Sveigðir	Reed Bringer
Svipall	Fleeting or Changeable
Sviðrir	Wise One
Sviðurr	Wise One
Svolnir	Cooler or Sweller
Thekkr	Clever or Pleasant One or Welcome One
Thrasarr	Quarreler or Raging, Furious
Thriði	Third
Thriggi	Triple
Thrór	Burgeoning or Inciter to Strife
Throttr	Strength
Thrundr, Þund	Sweller
Thunnr, Þuðr	Lean or Pale
Tveggi	Double
Tviblindi	Twice Blind
Unnr, Uðr	Beloved, Lover or Wave
Váði vitnis	Foe of the Wolf
Váfoðr, Vafuðr	Dangler, Swinger or:
Váfuðr	Wayfarer
Váfuðr Gungnis	Swinger of Gungnir
Vakr	Awakener or Vigilant
Valdr galga	Ruler of Gallows
Valdr vagnbrautar	Ruler of Heaven
Valföðr	Father of the Slain
Valgautr	Slain Gautr or Gautr of the Slain
Valkjosandi	Chooser of the Slain
Valtamr, Valtam	Slain Tame or The Warrior
Valtýr	Slain God
Valthognir	Slain Receiver
Vegtamr	Wayfarer or Waytamer
Veratýr	God of Men or God of Being
Viðrir	Stormer or Ruler of Weather
Viðrimnir	Contrary Screamer
Viðurr	Killer
Vingnir	Swinger

Vinr Lopts	Friend of Loptr
Vinr Lóðurs	Friend of Lóðurr
Vinr Míms	Friend of Mímir
Vinr stalla	Friend of Altars
Vodans	Master of Fury (Gothic)
Vofuðr	Dangler
Völsi	Lingam
Völundr rómu	Smith of Battle
Vut	Master of Fury (Allemanic, Burgundian)
Weda	Master of Fury (Frisian)
Wild Huntsman, Wilde Jaeger (German)	
Wise Victory Tree	
Wôdan	(*Proto-Western Germanic, OLG) Master of Fury
Woden	(Anglo-Saxon) Master of Fury
Wôðanaz	(*Protogermanic) Master of Fury
Wolfe	Wolf (German)
Wolf's Danger, The	
Wuotan/Wuodan	(Langobardic, Old High German)Master of Fury
Wunsch	Wish (German)
Yggiungr	(Terrible ?)
Yggr	Terrible One
Yrungr	Stormy

Appendix Five

List of Halls in Asgardhr

– Halls of Valhalla –

1. *Asgardhr* consisted of 12 or more realms, including Valhalla, home of Odhin; Thrudheim, home of Thor; and Breidablick, home of Baldr. Each Norse god had his own palace in Asgardhr. These lofty halls are reached from earth via Bifrost.

2. *Bilskirnir* - Thor's Hall meaning "Lightning"
Thor built his hall in the land called Trudvang (Thruthheim). The structure has 540 halls and is the largest building ever built in any of the Nine Worlds

3. *Breiðblikk* - Baldr's Hall meaning "Broadview"
No evil could enter the home of Baldur.

4. *Fensilar* - Frigga's Hall meaning "Halls of Water" or "fenlands"

5. *Folkvang* - Freyja's Hall meaning "Field of warriors" or "Field of folk"
In Folkvang there are nine castles. Freyja, as Valkyrie (choosers of the slain), brings her share of the slain warriors to her hall, Sessrumnir, "the many seated" where love songs are always playing. In the hall, the dead are catered to by faithful wives and women who died before marriage.

6. *Gladsheim* - Odin's Hall meaning "The Shining-Home" or "Place of Joy"
The home of the father of the gods, Gladsheim is located in Asgard, situated on the plain of Ida. It is the inner citadel or sanctuary of Asgard. Odin rules over the hall, but each of the twelve main gods also has a seat there.

7. *Valhalla* (the hall of the warriors killed in battle) is located within the hall.

8. *Glitnir* - Forseti's Hall meaning "Hall of Splendor"
This hall, the home of the god of justice, serves as a court where all legal disputes were settled. It has a roof made of silver that was supported by pillars of shining red gold.

9. *Helheim* - Hel's (Hella) Hall meaning "House of Hel"
Ruled by Hel, the daughter of Loki, the hall itself is called Eljudnir, home of the dead, and is located in Niflheim (one of the Nine Worlds, though sometimes Helheim and Niflheim are considered the same place). The entrance is guarded by Garm, a monstrous hound, and Modgud. It is cold and dark, with wind caused by the giant Hraesvelg (the corpse-eater) who sits at the edge of the world. No one can leave Helheim because the impassible river Gjoll flows from Hvergelmir and surrounds the hall. Even the gods are trapped if they enter. Those mortals who die of old age or sickness (and not in battle), or who do not worship a specific deity, go to Helheim after death.

10. Himminbjorg – Heimdals Hall meaning "Heaven hall"

11. *Landvidi* - Vidar's Hall meaning "White Land"
Spacious Hall , overgrown with branches and high grass.

12. *Noatun* - Njord's Hall meaning "shipyard"
It is at Noatun that Njord lives in a seaside palace.

13. *Sokkvabekk* - Saga's Hall meaning "Sunken Benches"
This is the abode of the "stream of time and events". Saga, the goddess of history, makes her home in Sokkvabaekk, and she and Odin drink there every day. It is here that she sings of gods and heroes.

14. *Thrymheim* - Skadi's Hall meaning "House of Uproar" of "Thunder-home"

Appendix Six

Etymology of Cain and Abel

The following extract edited from the referenced on-line source presents an opportunity for those intrigued by this perennial issue to study the root of language and thereby pursue the matter to their own satisfaction. The view that we, in the Clan hold regarding these brothers is expressed albeit briefly, elsewhere. All is ongoing, subject to change and adaptation.

"What is true today may not be tomorrow." [Roy Bowers]

Cain and Abel are known as Qáyin and Hével in their original Hebrew names. It is important to note that, because many traditions and later biblical narratives refer to them by different names. Cain was the first born, having been born in *Genesis* 4:1. It does not mention the duration of time between the birth of Cain and his younger brother, but Abel is born in the very next verse. We can only presume it was a minimum of nine months. The etymology behind Cain's name is derived from two different sources.

The original Hebrew word for Cain was *qanithi* (meaning 'to get'). Others speculate that the Cain's name comes from the Assyrian word *aplu* (meaning simply 'son'). The etymology for Abel's name is more relevant to his life. It was originally believed in English folk mythology that Abel's name derived from the words *ab* and *el*, which mean 'source of God.' This is a fallacy, however, because his original Hebrew name was not Abel, but rather Hével, which makes the letters incompatibly translated.

Abel's names is said to derive from a hypothetically reconstructed word meaning 'herdsmen,' which has the Arabic cognate *ibil*. Cain's name is said to derive from the mid-first-millennium BCE South Arabian (Yemen) word *qyn*, which was a word applied to a metal-smith. Hess contended that their names were merely descriptions of their roles in the *Genesis* narrative— their real names never really being known. By that logic, it can be decisively believed that Cain and Abel's real names were never known and that they were just given the names Cain and Abel (Qáyin and Hével) over the next millennia when *Genesis* was reconstructed, altered, and mistranslated.

Cain קין

Cain is the first son of Adam and Eve, the first human conceived and born, not created. He is said to be the first murderer of his brother Abel, the first human to die. For his deed, Cain is exiled and he flees to the land of Nod, East of Edin.

The name Cain is identical to the Hebrew word קין (*qyn*) meaning *spear*.

So from the Fates the gift of a spear was given to a fledgling race – destiny they placed within his grasp – how to sacrifice and what is worthy to offer, and the process of oblations were all of the Word, spoken through the 'Burning Stars' 'Flaming Shin,' the 'Fiery Bush,' the primal whisperings of the Hermit in the wilderness. We wander still.

ABOUT THE AUTHOR

Written by Shani Oates, in whose tradition of 'The People' she is Maid of the Clan of Tubal Cain. A published author, her substantial writings and musings on wide-ranging occult themes are transmitted into four books via Mandrake of Oxford, whose titles are: '*Tubelos Green Fire*'; '*The Arcane Veil*'; '*The 'Star Crossed Serpent*' (Volumes I & II, Vol. III forthcoming); as Guest author in '*Hekate: Her Sacred Fires*' by Avalonia Press and in '*The Wanton Green*' by Mandrake of Oxford and finally '*Abraxas II*' by Fulgur. Her other works have also appeared in various Pagan and occult journals and magazines including *The Cauldron, The Pentacle, The Wytches Standard, Verdelet, White Dragon, Pendragon, Hedge Wytch, Goddess Alive* and *Brigid's Fire*

Notes and References:

i Northumbria was created when twin kingdoms of Deira and Bernikia coalesced under considerable dispute during the 6th century. Raedwold of Anglia eventually defeated the kings of the North, drawing them into the aegis of Mercia. Northern Chronicles [wiki]

ii Ida is recorded within Greek linear A tablets. wiki

iiiAs a real place: In modern use, a municipality in northern Greenland (Avannaa) was formerly named Thule after the mythical land.

It is a rather sad inclusion here to note the appropriation of this archaic land and its beautiful mythos, arcane by thousands of years before its corruption at the hands of extreme despots whose political posturings presented a pseudo- historical version of Thule/Hyperborea to correlate it to their propaganda enforced concept of origins. The 'Oera Linda Book' allegedly 'found' by Cornelis Oera de Linden during the 19th Century was translated into German in 1933 and though much favoured by Heinrich Himmler has since been thoroughly discredited.iii And yet the principles and history that underpins this work, is accurate. Tenets of real history including, rune-lore, mysticism, arcane devotions concluded this most clever fiction.iii Specifically it records the current race of mystics as having evolved since the flood... hence Tubal Cain and Roy's interest in this date and the events surrounding it.

ivsuch as Orosius (384-420 A.D) and the Irish monk Dicuil (late 8th and early 9th century)

vWiki - Thule

vi Wiki

[vii] The Welsh form of her name is Gwenhwyfar possibly means 'White Spectre' and again shares commonalities with the Irish sovereignty goddess Findabair. viz. Aillil. Aillil, like

Welsh ellyll, means a fairy or sprite. The corresponding English word is, of course, elf (fr. OE aelf, akin to MHG alp, L. albus, "white"). [wiki]

[viii] [Mab, Mabh, Medb, Medhbh, Maeve] = mead

[ix]Etymology of Drighton*: Druhtinaz*

Old English: *dryhten*; Old Norse: *dróttinn*; Old English-Middle English: *drihten*; Middle English:*driȝten*) (Low German*Drost*, Early Modern Bavarian German:*Trecht* Lord God; New High German*(Kriegs-) Trechtein* 'military officer'). A common Germanic term that denotes a military leader or warlord derived from **druhti* 'war band' and the 'ruler suffix' *-īna-*(c.f.*Wōd-īna-z*). Proto-Germanic:*druhtīnaz'*

- Old English: *dryhten*
- Old Norse: *dróttinn*
- Old English-Middle English: *drihten*
- Old Saxon: *drohtin*
- Old Frisian: *drochten*
- Old High German: *truhtin*

Austro-Bavarian German/German: Trechtein(meaning Lord, Officer); *Kriegstrechtein* (military officer)

MiddleEnglish: *driȝten, driȝtin, drihtin, drightinn, drightun, driȝtyn, dryȝt(t)yn, driȝtine, drightin(e, dryghtyn(e, drichtine, driht(e, dryght, drichte, dright(e, drytte, dryȝt(e*

Reflexes of *druhti* are found inIcelandic:*drótt*, Old English:*dryht, driht*, Old High German:*truht*up into 19th century Swiss Germanas *Trucht* - ruffians, scallywags (as in dirty *rascal*? The priest as contender for the 'crown').

In Gothic appears the verb *driugan* meaning 'to do military service.'

In Old English *dréogan* (Modern English *drudge/drudgery*, and dialectal *dree*).

In Icelandic *drýgia(n)* appear, both meaning 'to perform.' (Hrothgar's wife in Beowulf, performs the sacred Mead ceremony) The root is the same as in Slavic *drug* meaning 'companion' (see druzhina).

[x] Note: In the Border countries, the name for this archetype was Gyre-Carling whose name had variants such as Gyre-Carlin, Gy-Carling, Gay-Carlin amongst others. Gyre is possibly a cognate from the Norse gýgr meaning "ogress"; carling or carline is a Scottish and Northern Englsih word meaning "old woman" which is from, or related to, the Norse word kerling -of the same meaning.

[xi] The Old Norse belief in disir, fylgjur and vordar ("follower" and "warden" spirits, respectively)typify arcane beliefs in ancestor origins. [wiki]

[xii] The Erlking (German: Erlkönig, "Alder King") is depicted in a number of German poems and ballads as a malevolent creature who haunts forests and carries off travellers to their deaths. But this 18th-century mistranslation of the original Danish wordelverkonge - "elf-king"/ Erlking is a character whose origins within common European folklore are sourced form the archetypal seductive but deadly faerie orsiren. Its original form in Scandinavian folklore of a female spirit is the elf-king's daughter (Elverkongens datter). Similar stories existed in numerous ballads throughout Scandinavia in which anelverpige (female elf) was responsible for ensnaring human beings to satisfy her desire, jealousy or lust for revenge.

Johann Gottfried von Herder introduced this character into German literature in Erlkönigs Tochter, a ballad based on the Danish folk legend about old burial mounds as the residence of the elverkonge, dialectically elle(r)konge, the latter has later been misunderstood in Denmark by some antiquarians as "alder king", cf Danishelletræ "alder tree". It has generally been assumed that the mistranslation was the result of error, but it has also been suggested (Herder does actually also refer to elfs in his translation) that he was imaginatively trying to identify the malevolent sprite of the original tale with a woodland demon (hence the alder king).

The story portrays Sir Oluf riding to his marriage but being entranced by the music of the elves. An elf maiden, in Herder's translation the Elverkonge's daughter, appears and invites him to dance with her. He refuses and spurns her offers of gifts and gold. Angered, she strikes him and sends him on his way, deathly pale. The following morning, on the day of his wedding, his bride finds him lying dead under his scarlet cloak. [wiki]

[xiii]Northumbria was created when twin kingdoms of Deira and Bernikia coalesced under considerable dispute during the 6th century. Raedwold of Anglia eventually defeated the kings of the North, drawing them into the aegis of Mercia. Northern Chronicles [wiki]

[xiv] Ida is recorded within Greek linear A tablets.

[xv] Bernikia /Bernicia:(OE): Bernice, Beornice; Latin: Bernicia) An Anglo-Saxon kingdom established by 6th century migrants in what is now Southeast Scotland and Northeast England. Bernicia is mentioned in the 9th century *Historia Brittonum* under many variants (*Berneich, Birneich, Bryneich* or *Brynaich.*). Anglian settlers would then have chosen one of these closest to their own tongue, to become either *Bernice* or *Beornice* in Old English.

[xvi]wiki

[xvii] [Cartimandua or Cartismandua (ruled c. 43 – 69)]

[xviii] Kings of Bernicia, (See also List of monarchs of Northumbria)

- Ida 'son' of Eoppa (547–559)
- Glappason of Ida (559–560)
- Addason of Ida (560–568)

- Æthelric son of Ida (568–572)
- Theodricson of Ida (572–579)
- Frithuwald (579–585)
- Hussa (585–593)
- Æthelfrith (593–616)
- Ida reigned, being followed by six sons, all rulers of Bernicia

[xix] Sacred Texts: Rig Veda:xxvii

[xx] A Dictionary of Vedic Rituals by Chitrabhanu Sen

[xxi] David Kinsley '*Hindu Goddesses.*' p15

[xxii] Harmoad, Mountain of Assembly, by O. D. Miller. P205

[xxiii] Gods, Sages and Kings, by David frawley, 1999 . Molital Banarsidass. p277

[xxiv] Miller p17

[xxv] Library, www.clanoftubalcain.org.uk

[xxvi] Frawley. p227

[xxvii] Frawley.p276

[xxviii] God of fire and acceptor of sacrifices. Agni is a messenger from and to the other gods, the link between heaven and earth. He is ever-young, an immortal. Agni, the Vedic god of fire, has two heads, one marks immortality and the other marks an unknown symbol of life. With Varuna and Indra, he forms a supreme triad, recorded in the Rig Veda. His vehicle is the ram.

[xxix] Indra: 'The God' of War, Storms, and Rainfall and who embodies the power of the primordial. He is celebrated as a demi-urge who pushes up the sky, releases dawn (Ushas) from the Vala cave, and slays V[illegible]tra; both latter actions are central to the Soma sacrifice. He has many epithets, including the bull, and the bountiful. Indra appears too as a god who embodies victory. The Rig-Veda states: *"He under whose supreme control are horses, all chariots, the villages, and cattle; He who gave being to the Sun and Morning, who leads the waters, He, O men, is Indra"* (2.12.7, trans. Griffith)

[xxx] Impeller = a person or thing that impels a rotar for transmitting motion [Centrifugal force]. Expeller = a force to drive out, discharge, deprive, extract. [Centripetal force].

[xxxi] [Wiki]

[xxxii] Notes

[xxxiii] See Appendix 3

[xxxiv]□ostre derives from Proto-Germanic *austr□, ultimately from aPIEroot*au□es-, 'to shine' and is closely related to a conjectural name of Hausos, the dawn goddess,*$h_2$aus□s, which would account for Greek Eos, Roman Aurora and Indian Ushas.

[xxxv]wiki

[xxxvi]Ibid.

[xxxvii]Beowa, Beaw, Beow, Beoor, Bedwigis an AS figure associated with barley and agriculture. Attested in the Anglo-Saxon royal genealogies in lineages carried back to Adam. Connections have been proposed between the figure of Beowa and the hero Beowulf and to the folk figure of John Barleycorn.

[xxxviii] *Interpretatio germanica*: the practice by the Germanic peoples of identifying Roman gods with the names of their own deities. Simek places this around the 1st century CE when both cultures cross-pollinated; examples occur in the days of the week as the Germanic translations of Roman deific terms describing them.

- The day of Marsis translated as the day of Ziu/Tyr (Tuesday).
- The day of Mercury is translated as the day of Wodan/Odhin (Wednesday).
- The day of Jupiter is translated as the day of Donar/Thor(Thursday), though Thor is generally identified in *interpretatio romana* as Hercules.
- The day of Venusis translated as the day of Friji/Frigg. (Friday)

Simek states:' that the problematic nature of *interpretatio germanica*is evident, and that divine attributes appear to have been the obvious factors for the correspondence between Jupiter and Thor, but for the other figures one must rely on speculation, and that far too little is known about what role the gods played in then-contemporary belief to be able to use their identification with particular Roman gods to trace their roles in later Norse myth.'

[xxxix] Ibid

[xl]The Well and the Tree The University of Massachusetts Press 1982 Amherst Paul C. Bauschatz

[xli] Robin the dart

[xlii] Wiki-Valkyries

- "Skögul's din" for "battlefield",
- "Gunnr's fire" for "sword" and
- "Hlökk's snow" for "battle",
- "Hildr's sail" for "shield" and

- "Göndul's crushing wind" for "battle", and
- "Göndul's din").

[xliii] Nafnapulur section of Skáldskaparmál contain an extended list of 29 Valkyrie names (listed as the 'Valkyries of Vidrir, an epithet of Odin). This provides the basic 24 + 5 vowels for the cardinals and centre, hence 25 +1+1 more. As they are known to 'shift' in threes, that makes eight sets of 3.

The first stanza lists: Hrist, Mist, Herja, Hlökk, Geiravör, Göll, Hjörþrimul, Guðr, Herfjötra, Skuld, Geirönul, Skögul, and Randgníð.

The second stanza lists: Ráðgríðr, Göndul, Svipul, Geirskögul, Hildr, Skeggöld, Hrund, Geirdriful, Randgríðr, Þrúðr, Reginleif, Sveið, Þögn, Hjalmþrimul, Þrima, and Skalmöld [wikipoedia]

[xliv]Alruna·Brynhildr·Eir·Geiravör·Göndul·Gunnr·Herfjötur·Herja·Hlaðguðrsvanhvít·Hildr·HervöralvitrVöluspá·Grímnismál·Darraðarljóð·Nafnaþulur·Hlökk·Kára·Mist·Reginleif·Róta·Sigrdrífa·Sigrún·Skögul and Geirskögul·Skuld·Svipul·Þrúðr [Ibid]

[xlv] The Old Norse poems Völuspá, Grímnismál, Darraðarljóð, and theNafnaþulur section of the Prose book Skáldskaparmál, provide lists of Valkyrie names. In addition, some Valkyrie names appear solely outside of these lists, such as Sigrún(who is attested in the poems Helgakviða Hundingsbana I and Helgakviða Hundingsbana II).

[xlvi]*Frau Holle, Frau Percht und Verwandte Gestalten* by Erika Timm,2003, (http://www.germanicmythology.com/original/earthmother.html) and http://www.germanicmythology.com/original/earthmother/odinswifebaldursmother.pdf

[xlvii] Terry Gunnel speaking of Bronze Age deities in http://www.germanicmythology.com/original/earthmother/odinswifenerthus.pdf

[xlviii] http://www.germanicmythology.com/original/earthmother/odinswifenerthus.pdf

[xlix] ibid

[l] Ibid.

[li]According to John McKinnell (2005), the development would be "Nerthus > *Njarðuz (breaking) > *Njörðuz (u-mutation) > Njörðr (synscope).

[lii] ibid

[liii] Ibid

[liv]http://www.germanicmythology.com/original/earthmother/odinswifebaldursmother.pdf

[lv] Ibid

[lvi] wiki

[lvii]The letter sequence, and indeed the letter inventory is not fixed. Compared to the letters of the rune poem given above, *f u þ o r cȝw h n i j eo p x s t b e m l ŋ œ d a æ y io ea*

The Thames scramasax has 28 letters, with a slightly different order, and *edhel* missing:

- f u þ o r cȝw h n i io eo p x s t b e ŋ d l m j a æ y ea
- The Vienna Codex has also 28 letters; the Cross inscription has 31 letters; Cotton Domitian A.ix (11th century) has another four additional runes:
- 30. cweorðkw, a modification of peorð
- 31. calc "chalice" k (when doubled appearing as kk)
- 32. stan "stone"st
- 33. gar "spear"g (as opposed to palatalized ȝ)
- These four additional letters are not found epigraphically (thestanshape is found on theWesteremden yew-stick, but likely as a Spiegelrune). Cotton Domitian A.ix reaches thus a total of 33 letters, according to the transliteration introduced above arranged in the order
- f u þ o r cȝw h n i j eo p x s t b e m l ŋ d œ a æ y ea io cw k st g

In the manuscript, the runes arranged in three rows, are replaced with Latin equivalents below (in the third row above) and with their names above (in the third row below). The manuscript has traces of corrections by a 16th century hand, inverting the position of *m* and *d*. Eolh is mistakenly labelled as *sigel*, and in place of *sigel*, there is a *kaun* like letter ᚴ, corrected to proper *sige*l ᛋ above it. Eoh is mis-labelled as eþel. Apart from *ing* and *ear*, all rune names are due to the later scribe, identified as Robert Talbot (died 1558). NB this note only from *wiki.*

[lviii] SPINNING IN MYTHS AND FOLKTALES by Thorskegga Thorn

[lix] Also sisters of Keres (black Fates),T hanatos (Death) and Nemesis (Indignation). Later they become the daughters of Zeus and the Titen, Themis - 'The Institutor' the embodiment of divine order and law, and sisters of Eunomia (lawfulness, order), Dike (Justice), and *Eir*ene (Peace). - [Wiki]

[lx] Ibid

[lxi]Etymology of Muse n. Muse Greek Mythology:

- Any of the nine daughters of Mnemosyne and *Zeus*, each of whom presided over a different art or science.
- *A guiding spirit.*

- A source of inspiration.
- A poet.

[Middle English, from Old French, from Latin M□sa, from Greek Mousa.]

Muse comes from Latin M□sa, from Greek Mousa. There are Greek dialect forms m□sa and *moisa*, and all three come from an original *montya. As to the further origins of this form, a clue is provided by the name of Mnemosyne, the goddess of memory and mother of the Muses. Her name is the Greek noun mn□mosun□ "memory," which comes from *mn□-, an extended form of the Greek and Indo-European root *men-, "*to think.*" This is the root from which we derive amnesia (from Greek), mental (from Latin), and mind (from Germanic). The reconstructed form *montya that is the ancestor of Greek Mousa could then mean something like "having mental power."

According to Pausanias, the Nine Muses have still older affinities. "The sons of Aloeus held that the Muses were three in number, and gave them the names of Melete (Practice) which could be either earth or fire, Mneme (Memory =air) and Aoede (Song= water)." - Wiki

Note: Hence the 9 are not only the nine muses but really 3 [graces] which is very useful in the context of a working compass. These equate very well with The Three Mothers...!

[lxii] "Zeusknows that his dearest Sarpedon will be killed byPatroclus, but he cannot save him. In the famous scene of Kerostasia, Zeus the chief-deity of the Myceneans appears as the guider of destiny. *Using a pair of scales* he decides that Hektor must die, according to hisaisa (destiny). His decision seems to be independent from his will, and is not related with any "moral purpose". His attitude is explained byAchilles topriam, in a parable of two jars at the door of Zeus, one of which contains good things, and the other evil. Zcus gives a mixture to some men, to others only evil and such are driven by hunger over the carth. This was the old "heroic outlook". - [Wiki]

[lxiii] Ibid

[lxiv] "Some [later] Greek mythographers went so far as to claim that the 'Moirai' were the *daughters of Zeus.* [despite the fact that] In the older myths they are *daughters of primeval beings like Nyx* ("Night") in Theogony, or Ananke ("Necessity") in Orphic cosmogony.

Whether or not *providing a father even for the Moirai* was a symptom of how far Greek mythographers were willing to go*, in order to modify the old myths to suit the patrilineal Olympic order*, the claim of a paternity was certainly not acceptable to Aeschylus, Herodotus or Plato." [Wiki] Note: Fatima, the daughters of Mohamed spring to mind here as prime examples of how the Mother becomes 'usurped' to become *daughters of the Father.*

[lxv] ibid

[lxvi] ibid

[lxvii] See the 'People of Goda' in Tubelo's Green Fire

[lxviii][Kveldulf Gundarsson, Tuetonic Magic, p. 24.]

[lxix] wiki

[lxx] Ibid.

[lxxi] ibid

[lxxii] wiki

[lxxiii]http://www.universetoday.com/21756/lupus/

[lxxiv] Ibid.

[lxxv] wiki

[lxxvi]Lexicon: Tyr/Tiw had become relatively unimportant compared to Odin/Woden in both North and West Germanic, and *specifically* in the sphere of organized warfare. Traces of the god remain, however, in Tuesday (Old English *tíwesdæg* "Tiw's day"; Old Frisian *tîesdei*, Old High German *zîestag*, Alemannic and Swabian dialect in south west Germany (today) *Zieschdig/Zeischdig*, Old Norse*týsdagr*), named after Tyr in both the North and the West Germanic languages (corresponding to *Martis dies*, dedicated to the Roman god of war and the father-god of Rome, Mars) and*Týviðr*, "Tý's wood", Tiveden may also be named after Tyr, or reflecting *Tyr*as a generic word for "god" (i.e., the forest of the gods). In Norway the parish and municipality of Tysnes are named after the god.

[lxxvii] See appendix 3

[lxxviii]Corresponding names in other Germanic languages are Gothic *Teiws*, Old english *Tīw* and Old high German *Ziu* and *Cyo*, all from Proto-Germanic **Tîwaz*(**Tē□waz*). The latinised name is *Tius* or *Tio*.

[lxxviii] Tyr became the Norweigen *Ty*, Swedish *Tyr*, Danish *Tyr*, extant as *Týr* in Modern Icelandic. The Old Norse name*Tyr* was a generic noun meaning 'god' and may be noted in the suffix to many of the epithets assigned to 'Odhin'. For example - *Hangatyr*, the 'god' of the hanged. Used in this way, the essence in the form of an emanation imbues another form.

[lxxix]Dyau□ group:

- Greek *Zeus*
- Roman *Iuppiter*
- Vedic *Dyau□ Pitār*
- *Dionysos (possibly)*, and Thracian *Sabazios* (from Saba Zeus?)

[lxxx]Deiwosgroup:

- Germanic*Tiwaz* (later known as Týr)
- Latin *Deus*
- Indo-Iranian *Deva/Daeva*
- Baltic *Dievas*
- Possible Slavic mythology *divu* (demons - meaning acquired from Iranian)[lxxx]
- Pronounced **di-ēus* (2 syllables) it became Latin *diēs*= 'day'
- Finnish and Estonian *taivas* and *taevas*, respectively, meaning 'heaven' or 'sky,' have probable source connections with Baltic *Dievas* or Germanic *Tiwaz*

[lxxxi] God of fire and acceptor of sacrifices. Agni is a messenger from and to the other gods, the link between heaven and earth. He is ever-young, an immortal. Agni, the Vedic god of fire, has two heads, one marks immortality and the other marks an unknown symbol of life. With Varuna and Indra, he forms a supreme triad, recorded in the Rig Veda. His vehicle is the ram.

[lxxxii] Indra: 'The God' of War, Storms, and Rainfall and who embodies the power of the primordial. He is celebrated as a demi-urge who pushes up the sky, releases dawn (Ushas) from the Vala cave, and slays V□tra; both latter actions are central to the Soma sacrifice. He has many epithets, including the bull, and the bountiful. Indra appears too as a god who embodies victory. The Rig-Veda states: *"He under whose supreme control are horses, all chariots, the villages, and cattle; He who gave being to the Sun and Morning, who leads the waters, He, O men, is Indra"* (2.12.7, trans. Griffith)

[lxxxiii]This one : B-bracteate of the B7 (IK 389), interpreted as depicting Frigga

[lxxxiv]http://members.aol.com/jordsvin/kindred/kindred.htm Reprinted from "Rainbow Wind" Magazine

[lxxxv]Britannia, the warrior queen, titan, valkyrie and disir, tutelary tribal deity and ultimately the national goddess of sovereignty. From Durga, through Athena, Brigantia/Bernikkia, the blazing coma, the starry crown atop the hair of Cosmic Fate.

[lxxxvi] Luwain is the main candidate for the language of the Trojans. Who despite their propensity for war, very much considered the female in high honour as prime force of heaven.

[lxxxvii]http://www.jtsa.edu/Documents/pagedocs/JANES/1980%2012/Arbeitman12. pdf p10-11

[lxxxviii]A *genderless* word that may have achieved an association with a 'male' deity through the *martyr*dom of Christ for the cause of humanity – a theme germane to the minds of all monks translating the Eddas and Sagas of those migrating People to these lands. It is also noteworthy to consider Tyr's Anglo-Saxon cognate as Tuisto is described in original tales as an hermaphrodite, which is enforced my modern linguistically analysis. [Rudolf Simek]

- martyr O.E., from L.L., from Gk. Martyr: in Christian use: "martyr, "lit." witness, "care, trouble, anxious, thoughtful, mindful and remember. "be anxious or thoughtful," [from PIE* (s) mrtu-cf. Skt. Smarati "remember," L. memor "mindful;"]

- mar·tyr [noun]: a person who is put to death or endures great suffering on behalf of any belief, principle, or cause....: a martyr to the cause of social justice.

[lxxxix]THING: The *'landstings'* authority was successively eroded after the island was occupied by the Teutonic Order in 1398. *Wiki.*

In late medieval times the 'Thing' was made up of 12 representatives for the farmers, free-holders or tenants. 12 + judge = 13 illegal attendees at a folk meeting!!! Not 'Sabbat' as in the cases of alleged and speculative witchcraft, but certainly heathens and heretics. The assembly of the thing was typically held at a specially-designated place, often a field or common, like *thingvellir*, the old location of the Icelandic thing.

[xc] See appendix 3

[xci] See appendices

[xcii]Shani Oates 'Od's man' http://www.clanoftubalcain.org.uk/odman.html

[xciii]Gavin Semple 'A Poisoned Chalice'
http://www.clanoftubalcain.org.uk/A_Poisoned_Chalice.pdf

[xciv]Doreen Valiente p117 Rebirth of Witchcraft' Hale 1989 London

[xcv] 'The Robert Cochrane Letters' by E.J. Jones; Ed Mike Howard. Capall Ban. UK 2002

[xcvi] DV p121

[xcvii] Ronald Hutton in Triumph of the Moon,

[xcviii] DV p122 Both these incidents may be explored in greater depth here.

[xcix] See Doreen Valiente. 'Rebirth of Witchcraft' Hale 1989 London

[c]Letter to Norman Gills

[lxiv]Mike Howard: The Magister of the Clan from 'The Robert Cochrane Letters' E. J. Jones 2002 Capall Bann. UK

[cii] E.J. Jones August 2000. Personal correspondence.

[ciii] E.J. Jones. Personal correspondence.

[xii] Extract of a poem from document/letter entitled 'The Basic Structure of the Craft' [Gills docs. Museum of Witchcraft. Box no.3344ABCDEF]

[cv] E.J. Jones August 2000. Personal correspondence.

[cvi] Cache of letters , newly released by John of Monmouth

[cvii] www.cyberwytch.com/roybowers

[cviii] Cache of documents, A1 circa 1961

[cix] Letters to Bill Gray?

[cx] Ibid. A3, circa 1962

[cxi] R of W. DV. 198? p?

[cxii] Anonymous poem written by a Clan member, described by RB in a letter to NG. Box 32 Boscastle

[cxiii] 'The Robert Cochrane Letters' by E. J. Jones and M. Howard. Capall Bann. 2002 p108

[cxiv] SMSD, ed Chas Clifton. 1998 USA pp 156,159-160

[cxv] E.J. Jones Personal correspondence. 1998

[cxvi] November 1998, private correspondence.

[cxvii] August 2000, Personal correspondence.

[cxviii] See their excellent website resource: http://ronaldchalkywhite.org.uk/

[cxix] See the Official 1734 Website: http://www.1734-witchcraft.org/

[cxx] The Cauldron # 103 Nov 2003

[cxxi] 23rd August 1996, Personal correspondence

[cxxii] [ibid]

[cxxiii] 6th September 1996 [ibid]

[cxxiv] See p93 'Sacred Mask Sacred Dance' Llewellyn Pub. 1997. USA

[cxxv] September 2000, Personal correspondence

[cxxvi] November 1999, Personal correspondence

[cxxvii] September 2001, Personal correspondence

[cxxviii] Doc 'T' – Cache of previously unpublished material.

[cxxix] May 1999 Private correspondence.

[cxxx] July 2000 . Personal correspondence.

[cxxxi] Ibid.

[cxxxii] July 2003 Personal correspondence.

[cxxxiii] 13th October 98. Personal correspondence.

[cxxxiv] Copy of Letter in personal possession.

[cxxxv] 'The Craft Today – Pentagram Nov. 1964 Robert Cochrane.

[cxxxvi] 'St Uzec' by Shani Oates : www.clanoftubalcain.org.uk/library

[cxxxvii] 'Ciphers and symbol' by Robin-the-dart: www.clanoftubalcain.org.uk/library

[cxxxviii] 'The Alchemy of the Compass' – Tubelo's Green Fire by Shani Oates. Mandrake of Oxford. 2010

[cxxxix] Note: possible reference source for Roy's 'Three Queens' of the Compass

[cxl] Notes

[cxli] **Author:**Monier-Williams, Monier, Sir, 1819-1899 **Subject:**Sanskrit language -- Dictionaries English **Publisher:**Oxford Clarendon Press **P368/9**

Online resources consulted:
http://www.pantheon.org/areas/mythology/

http://www.cybercomm.net/~grandpa/mythlogya.html

http://www.ugcs.caltech.edu/~cherryne/myth.cgi/Figures.html

http://everything2.com/title/The+Halls+of+the+Norse+Gods

http://www.reference.com/browse/wiki/Asgard

http://www.sacred-texts.com/neu/pre/index.htm

The Prose Edda, translated by Arthur Gilchrist Brodeur, at http://www.sacred-texts.com.

2472896R00090

Printed in Great Britain
by Amazon.co.uk, Ltd.,
Marston Gate.